W9-DDM-412

CATECHETICS
FROM A TO Z

CATECHETICS
FROM A TO Z

JACK and ARLENE WRIGLEY MURPHY

AVE MARIA PRESS   Notre Dame, Indiana

NIHIL OBSTAT   Rev. Msgr. Thomas P. Ivory
Censor Librorum

IMPRIMATUR   Most Rev. Peter L. Gerety, D.D.
Archbishop of Newark
March 1, 1982

ACKNOWLEDGMENTS

Unless otherwise noted, scripture texts are from THE JERUSALEM BIBLE,
copyright ©1966 by Darton, Longman & Todd, Ltd. and Doubleday and Company, Inc.

Excerpts from SHARING THE LIGHT OF FAITH, National Catechetical Directory
for Catholics of the United States, copyright © 1979, by the United States
Catholic Conference, Department of Education, Washington, D.C.,
are used by permission of copyright owner. All rights reserved.

International Standard Book Number: 0-87793-250-6

Library of Congress Catalog Card Number: 82-70787

Printed and bound in the United States of America.

COVER AND TEXT DESIGN   Carol A. Robak

PHOTOGRAPHY
Peter Aitken, 114 top
Alan R. Bagg, 114 bottom
Paul Conklin, 110
Bob Herbert, 64 bottom
Brent Jones, 8 bottom
William Koechling, 8 top
Carolyn McKeone, 34 bottom
Joanne Meldrum, 28, 94 bottom, 124 bottom, 132 top
Paul M. Schrock, 4, 50, 74, 90, 102 bottom, 146
James L. Shaffer, 16 bottom, 34 top, 64 bottom, 80 bottom, 94 top, 150 top
Bob Simmons, 80 top
Bob Taylor, 124 top, 140
Jim Whitmer, 16 top, 102 top, 132 bottom, 150 bottom

To our daughters,
Lauren Marya and Kristin Leavell,
and their grandfather,
Alexander Wrigley

CONTENTS

D

E

F

G

H

I

J

K

L

M

N

O

P

Q

R

S

T

U

V

W

Y

Z

INTRODUCTION

Jesus' most common title was *teacher*. In the four gospels Jesus is addressed or referred to as *teacher* almost 50 times. Jesus communicated the good news by teaching in the synagogues, by sharing his message wherever groups gathered around him and by telling stories to those who would hear him. *Teacher* is an honorable and respected title, and the catechists who teach are the people to whom we direct this book. We want to help them teach as Jesus did.

How did Jesus teach? He told stories, used examples from the experiences of the people he was with and taught them his way through his life. He used the best teaching methods of his day. This handbook is meant to assist teaching catechists of today to do the same—to use the best teaching methods and techniques of our times to share the message.

Catechesis is not only the transmission of Christ's message; it is also helping other people to meet Christ and to act upon that encounter. It requires communication.

All teachers, of course, are faced with the problem of acquiring and continually developing communication skills. Some teachers seem to know the techniques of communication naturally; others discover them haphazardly; still others, unhappily, never understand them.

In our work with teacher-catechists we often found that they did not have a common vocabulary, adequate guidelines in the area of educational theory, or sufficient resource information. We met volunteers, bright and competent in their own fields, closed out by some catechetical and educational language, a language meant to communicate ideas, methods and resources helpful to their efforts as teachers. And, although the bishops have emphasized the role of social sciences in catechetics, we have not found a workable handbook that provides the best thinking of secular and religious educators for our teachers, many of whom are dedicated volunteers.

We asked teacher-catechists whom we have worked with over the years to help us select the topics that they want to know more about. From a survey sent to over 100 teacher-catechists, we compiled a list of more than 500 themes. From that list we chose the topics that appeared most frequently in the survey and which reflected the questions of the many people we have worked with in parishes, at religious education workshops, at Catholic University in Washington, D.C., and in the New York metropolitan area. We thank all those who patiently responded to our surveys and questionnaires and helped us in many ways to arrive at the book *Catechetics From A to Z.*

We want to provide a concise source of ideas and suggestions on concepts and vocabulary, on resources, on accepted practices and techniques for the classroom. In brief, we want to give teachers a manual that goes with them into a classroom situation, a handbook that can help them grow as effective communicators of the good news.

Catechetics From A to Z is a way of looking anew or again at an important ministry: the day-by-day teaching of the message of Jesus.

HOW TO USE THIS BOOK

Catechetics From A to Z is meant to serve as a handbook with topics and themes arranged in alphabetical order for easy access. As the title also suggests, it is a basic resource for teacher-catechists. Its goal is to help teacher-catechists in their ministry and, especially, to help them implement the directives given in "Sharing the Light of Faith," the *National Catechetical Directory* (referred to as the *NCD* throughout the text).

Catechetics From A to Z is not a dictionary of definitions, but rather a concise manual with descriptive and informative essays geared to anyone involved in the religious education program. Topics include catechetics, methodology, educational psychology, resources, techniques and many others. This book can be used with catechetical preparation programs, in-service training sessions or as a reference for parish staff.

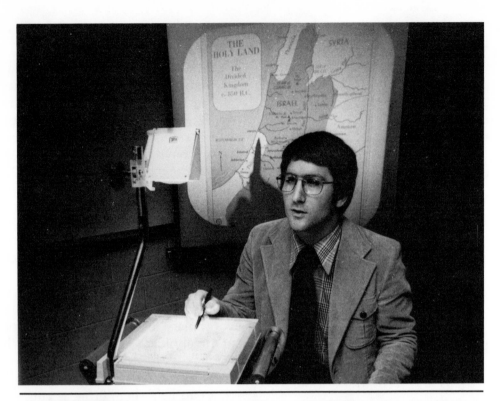

A

On the following day as John stood there again with two of his disciples, Jesus passed, and John stared hard at him and said, "Look, there is the lamb of God." Hearing this, the two disciples followed Jesus. Jesus turned round, saw them following and said, "What do you want?" They answered, "Rabbi,"—which means Teacher—"where do you live?" "Come and see" he replied (Jn 1:35-38).

A

ADMINISTRATION

Good catechetical programs invariably have a corps of dedicated, interested, prepared and responsive teachers. Also characteristic of these programs is a good administration providing support, encouragement, facilities, supplies and resources. It is evident that administrators of long-term programs, parish or diocesan, have given time and thought to building the structures in which these programs operate.

Diocesan directors of religious education offer services and resources to parishes through teacher-training programs, workshops, congresses, regional resource centers for texts and audio-visual materials. Diocesan directors coordinate the many programs in the area and promote interaction among them. Obviously it is important to provide services that are well-organized, conveniently scheduled, adequately presented and available to the largest number practical and possible. Good communication is essential at the diocesan level.

On the parish level the director of religious education, the DRE, is responsible for well-organized facilities, supplies, resources, ideas, staff interaction, supervision and cooperation with other parish programs and personnel. The DRE serves as liaison between the parish program and the diocesan office of religious education.

In 1978 *The National Inventory of Parish Catechetical Programs* showed that in practice DREs gave the most effort to planning curricula and programs, teaching religion, providing materials and coordinating in-service teacher training.

Administration is most effective when it provides services to people. *To administer* means "to serve," not "to rule or direct." The *NCD* points out that "effective planning is person-centered" and "does not propose structures without reference to the people involved." Good administration helps teaching catechists function creatively and effectively.

See also DIRECTOR OF RELIGIOUS EDUCATION, GRADE-LEVEL COORDINATORS and ADVISORY BOARD.

ADOLESCENTS

Say the word *adolescents* and many teachers think of teen-agers, those difficult and peculiar young people, students "most likely to be avoided" by the parish. This is the group for whom all catechetical time and effort seem to produce the least evident results.

Fortunately we are becoming more aware of what it means to be an adolescent in terms of human development and of Christian life. The *NCD* calls the years between 12 and 18 "an age of religious crisis," the time "when many young people either begin to abandon the faith of their childhood or become more deeply committed to it" (No. 199b).

According to psychologists it is a time of identity crisis, discovery, exploration, acceptance, rejection and confusion. Resolution comes only through crisis and struggle.

Human growth during the adolescent period involves radical physical, psychological, emotional, intellectual and spiritual changes. Oddly enough, all this change is normal. Teacher-catechists face the difficulty of working with volatile and often unpredictable behavior. It is extremely hard to work with such continuously changing people. This period, however, is critical since it is a transition time for the emergence of adult faith.

Youth ministers and catechists can gain insight into adolescent behavior from such writers as Erik Erikson. Erikson describes eight stages of human growth, placing adolescents in a stage where major issues are identity and identity confusion. The adolescent's critical task, according to Erikson, is the definition of self, of who he or she is. Adolescents develop this sense of identity from the way they see themselves and the way they are perceived by those important to them. They want to belong to groups that will help them find themselves.

Ronald Goldman, an English educator-psychologist, points out that in the movement from childhood to adult life the adolescent characteristically rejects and seeks anew. There is an "increasing sense of unreality and irrelevance of religious teaching as childhood is left behind and adolescents begin to think for themselves." They ask their own questions about who and what they are.

We cannot solve the problems of adolescents in the church by simply suggesting that they are being difficult and wishing they would return to the devotion of their younger days.

As the *NCD* points out, a special youth ministry is critical, and curriculum material and programs must be considered in terms of the social and personal development of the adolescents.

See also YOUTH MINISTRY, HIGH SCHOOL PROGRAMS and DEVELOPMENTAL PSYCHOLOGY.

ADULT EDUCATION

Jesus' efforts as a teacher were primarily geared to the adults of the communities he visited. He taught in the temple, on the hillside, and by the lake. Children were present and experienced the time with Jesus, but he directed his words to the adult population.

Much of today's religious education is directed to programs for children. Unfortunately "adult education" too often means a lecture series or course given during the six weeks of Lent. In some parishes meetings scheduled for the parents of first communicants are considered adult education.

The *NCD* speaks of adult catechesis in terms of "small group discussions, lectures with questions and discussion, retreat programs, sacramental programs, dialogue between adults and young people, adult catechumenate" (No. 225).

Many critical thinkers in religious education today question whether or not adult education/catechesis isn't in reality still an appendage of special events in the parish. The emphasis remains on programs for children. The issue for some writers is: Shouldn't we be running *adult-centered* programs where the norm is continuous growth in understanding and practice for the entire community, and where learning is actually lifelong?

In 1977 a United States Catholic Conference symposium produced a set of goals for adult education:

1) to aid individuals to discover and to develop their potentials as persons created in the image of God;

2) to recognize the meaning of life and to respect it in all its dimensions;

3) to incorporate the message of Jesus into one's personal life;

4) to articulate and to share the teaching of Jesus with others;

5) to understand and reflect upon the "signs of the times" so as to give direction to change in order to shape the future;

6) to provide opportunities for ongoing learning at all periods of adult life;

7) to participate in and celebrate life in the church, the community of believers;

8) to aid committed Christians to serve the needy, the outcast, the discriminated against and the segregated.

These goals call for programs that go beyond hearing the word in the liturgy. They demand an ongoing, systematic attempt to provide direction, information and support for the adult Christian.

One change in the post-Vatican II community may be the emergence of lay people; hence the need for a more broadly based "school of religious thought and practice." We have popularly and traditionally held that once children were taught, they would never leave the church; frequently they also remained "children" in the church. The call to personal freedom and adulthood in the faith demands a new catechesis.

ADVENT

Advent, the beginning of the liturgical year, is the church's first teaching device. The presence of Jesus—past, present and to come—is proclaimed in the words, the music and colors of the church. This season begins with the Sunday that falls closest to November 30, the feast of Saint Andrew the Apostle.

Teaching catechists can find this season a marvelous treasure. The readings about John the Baptist preparing the way of the Lord; the words of Isaiah, the prophet; the promises of hope, salvation and freedom are beautiful and moving. The 1969 revision of the liturgical year gives a three-year cycle for the lectionary that provides a wide range of readings. Cycle A takes most of its readings from Matthew; Cycle B draws upon Mark; and Luke provides much of Cycle C. Each year during late Lent and Eastertime the readings are from John. The catechetical journals usually provide the readings for the Sundays in Advent and for the feast of the Immaculate Conception (December 8) which falls during Advent. They offer lessons for related activities. (See PERIODICALS.)

The Advent themes of waiting and preparing, of hopefulness and anticipation, and the customs of the Jesse tree, the Advent wreath and calendar, all provide teachers with curriculum material that can be translated into classroom experiences. Teaching Advent hymns, taken from the parish hymnbook, prepares students to participate in the Advent liturgies. The traditional Angelus is a good Advent prayer, praising and teaching in one voice.

The season of Advent is a real challenge to teachers and parents. It comes now in company with a commercial blitz of Santa Claus, elves, snowmen, reindeer and winter festivals. Many children spend their Advent waiting-time in line to see Santa and anticipating Christmas surprises. Their parents are waiting too, in other lines, to pay for Christmas gifts.

While these four weeks can be difficult for teachers, there are many practical and workable suggestions available in various texts and in the catechetical journals that come out in the late fall. Efforts to focus on the true meaning of Advent must be made through classroom activities, community Advent practices, well-prepared liturgies and family cooperation.

Advent is a hectic time for many adults and a time of confusion for children. Teachers must keep in mind, however, that Advent is the *only way* to prepare for Christmas.

A helpful resource for teacher-catechists is a study guide and handbook that are included in a packet of parish Advent material produced by Alternatives, a non-profit group. (Alternative Christmas Campaign, P.O. Box 1707, Forest Park, GA 30050.)

See also CHRISTMAS.

ADVISORY BOARD

A significant change today is the renewal of the concept of ministry. There has been a shift away from the separateness of ordination and religious consecration to a shared ministry of all members of the community.

In this context the work of catechesis needs to be more broadly based and structured to allow the many voices of the community to be heard formally and effectively. Curriculum choices, text selection, program policy, parent involvement and cooperation are no longer issues determined solely by the priest-moderator or the DRE. A shared responsibility for catechetical programs is beginning to evolve.

What has begun to emerge is an Advisory Board for the entire catechetical program. These boards are not too dissimilar from the Confraternity of Christian Doctrine Boards that operated from the 1930s to the 1960s. The CCD Boards pioneered a lay involvement in the catechetical movement that was characteristically American in its cooperative sharing of responsibility. In practice, lay people under a priest-moderator assumed decision-making roles in all aspects of the CCD program — teaching on the elementary and high school levels, adult education, parent programs, attendance and clerical work.

The Advisory Board approach is still not part of many parish programs. When it does exist, it generally consists of a representative from the rectory, a representative from the convent (if sisters are present and active in catechetical work), the DRE, elected delegates from the teaching staff and parents.

Many boards have developed a constitution to establish policy and ensure continuity in catechetical programs. Changing of key persons in a program should not change policy established by the community. Change should result from community needs and development and not from the personality of a new DRE or priest-moderator.

The Advisory Board may be one of the most visible signs of a viable religious education program; it takes the theory and practice of a community of believers seriously. It trusts the Spirit operating in and through this community.

AFFECTIVE EDUCATION

The *NCD* calls attention to an interesting methodology by encouraging catechists "to reach the whole person, using both cognitive (intellectual) and affective (emotional) techniques" (No. 176).

"Emotional techniques?" one might ask. The word *emotional* often conveys thoughts of sentimentality or of feelings that are out of control. What could this emotional "stuff" have to do with teaching?

There is more to education than intellectual achievement. Affective education, the emotional well-being of students, is also an important part of the educational process. It includes the confidence students develop about their own abilities, their relationships with others, their willingness and ability to express themselves, their development of a value structure and their attitude formation. Affective education emphasizes the role of the emotions in the learning process.

Some of the affective approaches that can be utilized by religious educators are procedures that help students take moderate risks, make decisions, use feedback and assess their own progress; methods that use personal experiencing as a means of stimulating personal growth, such as imaginative role plays and drama; opportunities for students to examine the meaning and personal impact of their experiences; methods used for valuing, such as values clarification; techniques for fostering attitudes.

Jesus was an affective teacher before a title was given to the process. He related to the whole person and was very conscious of the emotional well-being of those he was with. Jesus taught values and communicated attitudes.

See also VALUES CLARIFICATION and EXPERIENTIAL APPROACH.

AGING

*Learning is ever in the freshness of
its youth,
even for the old.*

—Aeschylus

The aged, in earlier times, were a very small minority of the population. Today we have a larger percentage of older people, many of whom are healthy and active members of the community. "Gray power," "leisure worlds," "golden-agers," and "senior citizens," are all terms that remind us that the aged among us are not only present but active. Has the catechetical movement taken this group into consideration?

There is certainly a growing concern in the church community for the aged, but much of it is centered on the sacrament of the anointing of the sick or the needs of the lonely and sick. But the aging population today is not exclusively the "almost dying" one. We have a group of people who retire earlier, who are frequently eager to do something for the church community, and who have developed the resources to contribute to many areas of parish life. The needs—and talents—of this group should be considered in religious education programs.

The aging are a major resource for personnel in all positions. As more women join the full-time work market, the traditional pool of volunteers is diminishing. Older people can take on many of these roles—teacher-catechists, aides, floating music or art teachers—as well as become involved in the planning and administrative aspects of the various programs.

Catechetical programs to meet the specific needs of the aged must be incorporated into the adult education programs. With retirement many older people have leisure time during the day when special activities, sessions and courses can be planned by them and for them.

See also ADULT EDUCATION, ANOINTING OF THE SICK and DEVELOPMENTAL PSYCHOLOGY.

AIDES

A teacher's aide, as the name implies, assists and provides services in the classroom. Teachers using the experiential approach find the added assistance of an aide valuable. An effective teacher's aide helps individualize, works with small groups, projects and discussions.

Aides are introduced into a program only after adequate preparation of both aide and teacher. Some teaching catechists, especially volunteers, feel uncomfortable with another adult in the room. The role of the aide in the classroom must be described to the faculty. Aides should be assigned only to those teachers who request them. Soon word-of-mouth reports help eliminate the fears and insecurities some teaching catechists initially feel.

Aides often begin by taking attendance, checking assignments, dealing with individual problems in the classroom, preparing and distributing materials, running audiovisuals and helping younger children with coats and boots when necessary.

As the teacher and aide continue to work together, the aide may play a greater role in the teaching-learning experience. Small-group discussions, skits and plays, tutoring and testing can all be handled by an aide. Aides are especially helpful on field trips because, unlike volunteer chaperones, they know all the children.

The DRE should provide ongoing programs for the development of aides. Training should include a presentation of the aims of the overall program, workshops on the use of audio-visual equipment, and discussions of materials available for each level. Aides should be included in the in-service program provided for teachers.

Working as a teacher's aide is a good introduction to teaching. Frequently these assistants become teaching catechists. They learn much about classroom management and teaching by firsthand observations. Under the direction of good teachers, aides who wish to assume more responsibility for the class begin a type of internship.

Of course adult aides should be invited to faculty meetings and be considered members of the staff. If student aides (such as high school students) are used, common-sense judgments about their role on the staff should be made.

ANOINTING OF THE SICK

Vatican II changed the name of the sacrament of extreme unction (last anointing) back to "the anointing of the sick." The name change expresses the shift in thinking about this sacrament of healing, this sign of Christian hope.

Generally the texts at the middle-grade level cover this sacrament. Today the emphasis has moved from a concentration on death and dying to a sacramental concern for all who are seriously ill and for the aged. As a corollary to the study of this sacrament, students should see the personal role of each Christian in service to the sick and the aged.

Catechesis for this rite should be based on the biblical stories of Jesus' healing and, of course, should be tied in with the resurrection theme. Many parishes encourage and provide communal celebrations of the anointing of the sick and the aging. What was in fairly recent times an exclusively private ceremony in a hospital room or by a sickbed can now also be a community experience in which the students can join in prayer and presence. This makes instruction in this sacrament much more meaningful and experiential and, of course, more personal.

One word of caution to teachers: Young children can be fascinated by the topics of death, dying and types of sickness. Avoid discussions of "eligibility requirements" for the reception of the sacrament with them. Many inexperienced teachers report being sidetracked in long discussions of symptoms, whether or not certain diseases are terminal, and so forth. Students should be aware that the sacrament of the anointing of the sick is not just for the dying, but neither is it administered to people with routine colds or other minor illnesses. Center instruction on Jesus, on his relationship with the infirm and his healing, not on the diseases.

ART PROJECTS AND ACTIVITIES

"I'm a religion teacher, not an art expert."

"After we get through with the *real* lesson, I'll let them color and draw."

"We have so much material to cover that I never have time for projects."

"When *I* was in second grade, everyone in the class knew all the commandments by heart. Of course we never wasted time with activities."

These objections to the use of art projects and activities in religious education come from a mistaken notion of learning, of children and of religious experience. The *NCD* tells us:

> From the very beginning, the Church has used the arts to communicate Christ's message and fix it in people's minds and hearts. Biblical stories, saints' lives, and religious themes of all sorts have been depicted in stained glass, mosaics, painting and sculpture (No. 251).

Many teacher-catechists, however, grew up with a different experience of religion classes—one that did not include the arts, especially at the *doing* level. The suggested art and activities in teacher's manuals reflect a newer approach. Experiential learning, student involvement, hands-on experiences, doing, active rather than passive learning is being recommended. And art is an ideal way of using this approach.

Many teacher-catechists hesitate to undertake art projects because they themselves are not "artistic." Much of this uncertainty can be removed if art is presented—to teachers *and* students—as a universal human activity in which the aim is expression, not perfection. Picasso, rediscoverer in his own work of a candor of expression that had been lost, was visiting an exhibition of children's drawings and commented: "When I was their age I could draw like Raphael, but it took me a lifetime to draw like them."

Teachers sometimes bypass meaning and the wonderful candor of children's art and encourage neatness, praise matching colors and admire coloring "in the lines."

Some common-sense guidelines will help ensure success in the classroom:

▸ Keep art projects simple.

▸ Try the project before presenting it to the class. This helps you in assisting the students and gives a realistic idea of how much time you should allot for the activity.

▸ Relate the art activity to the lesson. Connect the project with the exploration and examination of key ideas or concepts, expressing them in a form that inspires, teaches or extends the learner's grasp. In this sense simple freehand drawings may be more expressive and meaningful than coloring prepared pictures.

▸ Select projects appropriate to the developmental level and abilities of the students. For example, large muscles develop before smaller ones. Therefore preschoolers enjoy finger painting but are frustrated with coloring or painting an intricate, detailed picture.

▸ Encourage individual expression. Mass producing coloring-book pictures, tracing and copying should be kept minimal. Use more creative, freeform activities in which children can express their feelings and thoughts.

▸ Organize materials and supplies in advance. Be sure to have enough supplies for everyone.

▸ Vary the types of projects used. Sometimes a teacher sees how much students enjoy a particular project and repeats it too frequently.

Finger painting, clay sculpting, collages using easy-to-handle items, box building and decorating, pasting and cutting, sand expressions, freehand painting and coloring are the favorite activities of younger children. Since their attention span is short, it is better to plan projects that can be completed in one class session.

Older children enjoy group projects and activities that involve cooperation and competition. Among their favorite art projects are mosaics, montages and collages, shadowboxes, murals, papier-mâché, paper sculpture, string art, photography, building models, painting and freehand drawing. With middle-grade and older students, projects can be long-range, even continuing for several weeks.

Coloring books and coloring sheets are the least popular with both groups. Older students feel they are babyish, and younger ones are frustrated by them.

Many teacher's manuals and handbooks give complete directions for various art projects. Public libraries have arts-and-crafts books for suggestions and ideas.

See also BUSY-WORK AND GIMMICKS

AUDIO-VISUAL MATERIALS (description)

The use of AVs (audio-visual materials) is common in most religion classes today. AVs help the process of communication by presenting or reinforcing lessons through more than one sense. Another term used is multimedia material. The following list gives the equipment and materials commonly used by teachers.

Projectors

1) The *film projector*, or movie projector, is designed to show 16mm film with sound. The home movie projector is generally 8mm or super 8mm and little commercially prepared religious education material is available for that size.

2) The *filmstrip projector* is a simple machine to operate, projecting 35mm still pictures. Teachers can regulate the speed of the presentation, focus longer on a frame, add a commentary, use a record, or have students prepare explanations for each frame. Some projectors have a record-player attachment. These projectors can be purchased with automatic or manual change mechanisms.

3) The *opaque projector* projects and enlarges a page from a book, diagram or a chart onto a screen or wall. For an additional use of this projector, large sheets of paper can be taped to a wall. Then the picture, graph or map is placed on the machine, projected and traced on the paper to be used for bulletin or display purposes, or even for scenery.

4) The *overhead projector* projects a picture, graph, chart, illustration or writing on a screen *above* and *behind* the speaker's head. The teacher can face the group and talk while writing or underlining something on the transparency which is projected. (Overhead projectors cannot be used with books or other opaque materials.)

5) The *slide projector* is relatively easy to operate. Many families have their own slide projectors and teachers may be more familiar with this machine than any other. Slides, positive transparencies mounted in cardboard, are projected onto a screen.

Slide projectors range from the cheapest and simplest machines which hold only one slide at a time, to the carousel projectors which hold prepared arrangements of slides in order of showing. The latter is recommended for classroom use. A remote control cord switch is available on some models. This gives the teacher freedom to move away from the projector to be with the students.

Films and Transparencies

1) *Films* used in the classroom are generally 16mm, with or without sound, black-and-white or color. Religious-education films can be rented, bought or borrowed. Some AV companies periodically send parishes catalogs of films for rental or purchase. Many diocesan offices of religious education have film libraries. Public libraries also have films which may be useful in catechetical programs.

2) *Filmstrips* can be purchased in kits or can be made by the teachers themselves. Ready-to-use filmstrips come in sets complete with lesson plans, narration scripts, and records or tapes. Some sets include suggestions for grade-level adaptations and have spirit-master sheets for lesson extensions.

Filmstrips can be made by using 35mm slide film and requesting uncut processed slides when having them developed. One important caution: When making homemade filmstrips, you are limited to a vertical format. Be sure to hold the camera vertically.

3) *Slides* can be taken with any camera using slide film. A few publishers include commercially prepared slides in their catalogs. For material especially relevant to the parish program, however, groups of teachers, students or members of the parish can prepare slides. This project can be an effective learning experience as well as a practical way of updating the parish AV library.

4) *Transparencies* are clear plastic sheets about 8½ inches by 11 inches that can be purchased with prepared charts, maps, graphs and pictures, or blank so teachers can prepare their own material using felt-tip pens. An overhead projector is used to show transparencies on a screen or wall. Homemade transparencies can be erased and reused. They can be prepared in advance or written on during the presentation as easily as one writes at a desk. An *overlay* is a transparency which is laid on top of another to add information or detail as the presentation progresses.

Other Audio-Visual Materials

1) *Bulletin boards* are effective when the materials posted are changed as the lesson themes develop. Bulletin boards are also used to display students' work, to supplement information, to review materials and to offer visual alternatives to looking at the teacher or walls when students are bored. Students enjoy planning and preparing bulletin boards.

2) *Chalkboards* are often referred to as blackboards even though they come in other colors. This old-time visual aid has not lost favor in the classroom. Sometimes a chalkboard is used spontaneously during the course of a class to spell a word, to diagram a situation, and so forth. But a planned chalk talk, using stick figures or drawings to tell a story, adds life to a lesson or a lecture.

3) *Photographs, posters and designs* can stimulate the senses, provoke discussion or provide atmosphere in a room. Students enjoy sharing photographs of christenings or weddings when studying the sacraments.

4) *Records* are available with stories, songs, background music and classroom activities geared to religious education. Teachers can also use popular and classical music for teaching purposes.

5) *Cassette tape recorders* for sound reproduction are widely used. They are extremely valuable for songs, narrations, preparation of skits and the development of background music or sound. *Video cassettes* are attractive teaching aids but are not widely used in religious education yet.

6) *Television*. Some dioceses have already initiated closed-circuit television programming primarily for Catholic school programs. Hopefully, with the advance of the video cassette, some of this material will become available to the after-school or weekend programs.

AUDIO-VISUAL MATERIALS (use and abuse)
Films and Filmstrips

Any teacher who has ever had a projector bulb blow out after the first few minutes of a film, or has found that a film wasn't rewound from the last time it was used, or was surprised that the students didn't want to see another film, will appreciate the do's and don'ts of this list.

DO

1) Have all equipment ready to run. Check projectors and extension cords. Be sure that the film is in one piece, that it has been rewound and that there are extra projector bulbs.

2) Make sure you know how the equipment works.

3) Check the physical setup of the room for sufficient seating, adequate darkness, good ventilation, the location of the electric outlets and switches.

4) Know why you are showing a particular film. Preview it! Watch it in terms of your students and their needs.

5) Read any study guide or lesson plan that accompanies the film.

6) Prepare the students for what they will be seeing.

7) Know how long the film runs. Plan the session to include time for introducing, viewing and discussing the material. Remember, some films lend themselves to other activities such as role-playing, re-enactment or artwork. Build that time into your planning.

DON'T

1) Show a film or filmstrip simply because it is available.

2) Talk too much during the film or explain every scene to the class.

3) Show a film to fill in for an unplanned lesson or for an entertainment break.

4) Depend totally upon student help to run the equipment.

5) Show films or filmstrips too frequently. More is not better, and live dialogue is critical to good learning.

6) Show a film without allowing adequate time for evaluation and discussion. A 50-minute film, for example, is too long for a 60-minute period.

7) Forget to rewind the film after you preview it.

8) Expect a film to make up for poor teaching.

Slides, Posters, Charts, Multimedia Packets, Records, Tapes, Decorations, etc.

1) Be sure that posters, charts, pictures, flannel boards, and chalkboard illustrations are large enough to be seen from all parts of the room. Records and tapes must be loud enough and clear enough to be heard.

2) All audio-visual aids must be interesting to the students, in good taste, and not so obscure that you continually have to explain symbols or meanings.

3) If the audiovisual is to be part of the lesson, plan carefully how, when and where you will use it. Have it in a convenient place before class. Nothing destroys a lesson faster than stopping to find a poster or illustration, or having to set up a record player or tape at a critical point in the discussion or presentation.

4) Arrange slides before class. Students get restless, and sometimes even giddy, if the teacher has to figure out which slide is next or if slides must be adjusted because they were placed in the projector upside down or backwards.

5) Know how much time to allow for each slide. If the presentation is too fast, it may blur the meaning and idea of the picture; if it is too slow, the students become bored or restless. If possible, run through the lesson at home and ask for feedback.

6) Use the ready-made multimedia packages available today with the same cautions suggested for use of fast food and other convenience items. Remember that they're expensive and too much dependence on them causes an unbalanced diet!

7) Classroom decorations and displays should contribute to the learning atmosphere of the room, relate to the themes studied and, as often as possible, be prepared by the students. Remember that students' eyes travel all the time. Help them learn visually from bulletin boards, posters, charts, displays and decorated windows and doors.

B

"Go, therefore, make disciples of all the nations; baptise them in the name of the Father and of the Son and of the Holy Spirit, and teach them to observe all the commands I gave you. And know that I am with you always; yes, to the end of time" (Mt 28:19-20).

B

BAPTISM

The role of the catechist teaching children already baptized differs from the role of the catechist preparing catechumens according to the *Rite of Christian Initiation of Adults*, a major catechetical approach emphasized since the Second Vatican Council.

Baptism, for teaching catechists of the already baptized, is a sacrament of explanation and enrichment, not preparation. The direction is to nurture in all their students an understanding of the sacrament and personal renewal, to review with them what was done, and to help them through further study and experience to accept fully what was done for them as infants.

Children learn well by experience, and this sacrament provides an abundance of material to work with. Most students know something about baptism; many have pictures of their own baptism and have been to some younger relative's baptism. The baptismal font is usually visible in the church and accessible to religion classes. The signs and symbols of baptism offer topics for discussion, suggest art projects and designs. The liturgy for baptism can be dramatized by children of all ages.

The community experiences of children should also emphasize the communal aspects of the sacrament of baptism. In some parishes infant baptisms are celebrated at a Sunday eucharistic liturgy. Middle grade and older students should be able to share in the community celebration of the Easter Vigil and learn about the relationship of baptism to new life in Christ.

Children learn how they were "born again," made members of the church and "washed in the spirit" through stories from the Bible, from stories that Jesus told. At each level of development these lessons and stories take on fuller meanings.

A word relating to baptism that has come to the fore in recent times is *evangelization*, "bringing people to a personal commitment to Christ." The American bishops have pointed out that "inasmuch as children have been baptized in infancy on the basis of parents' faith, the 'evangelization of the baptized' becomes a necessary stage in the promotion of the faith." For many, nurturing the renewal of those already baptized through the study of the sacrament of baptism is following this evangelical thrust.

See also CATECHUMENATE and EVANGELIZATION.

BEATITUDES

A common complaint in many parishes is the lack of simply stated moral norms for children today. Some people long for the morality of an earlier age which seemed to make right and wrong easier to determine; they miss catechisms with clear and definite examples of mortal sins, or with carefully spelled-out rules for moral behavior.

The *NCD* wants morality to be taught "in light of the Ten Commandments, the Sermon on the Mount, especially the beatitudes, and Christ's discourse at the Last Supper" (No. 105). Most teacher-catechists know, however, that Jesus' beautiful words are complex, subtle and difficult; they require reflection, maturity and study. The teaching catechists' charge from the *NCD*, then, is to help children understand morality from the fullness of Jesus' teaching.

The beatitudes represent a particular challenge because they are difficult for young people to understand. Avoiding them or providing an adult exegesis is not the solution.

Jesus spoke the beatitudes to the adult community that day on the mount. It is from the actions of the adult community that even the youngest of the children will begin to learn the beatitudes.

These beginnings are later reinforced with classroom learning. Starting at the middle grade level with activities and prayer celebrations based on the words of Jesus is the best way to formally begin this study of morality. Start with vocabulary concepts already existing in the students' minds. Listen to their understanding of the beatitudes and help them refine and expand their insights, especially by referring to actual deeds of Jesus and his followers, to lives of saints and to people of today.

A good learning experience is to have the children write their own ideas of happiness in a form similar to the beatitudes. Then ask the students to relate their descriptions of happiness to the words of Jesus. (There is a lesson, an activity and a paraliturgy for middle-school students on the beatitudes in *Doing, Dance and Drama*, Ave Maria Press. Pflaum Resources has an eight-filmstrip set called *To Live as Jesus Did: The Beatitudes* for middle and upper-elementary classes.)

As children mature, teacher-catechists need to help them relate their insights and experiences to their understanding of the beatitudes. Teachers also need to understand the relationship of morality to development.

Teen-agers, often critical of adult ideals, will find these words of Jesus provocative and demanding and may well find answers to their own quest for truth and justice.

See also DEVELOPMENTAL PSYCHOLOGY, MORAL DEVELOPMENT and COMMANDMENTS.

BIBLE

In terms of the catechetical renewal, perhaps the key emphasis has been on the scriptures, the reopening of the Bible. Each new religion text calls upon students and teachers to read, to reflect and to pray the Bible. Teacher training stresses understanding and knowledge of the Bible.

Some cautions are necessary, however, about what students can and cannot do with the Bible. Children of preschool and early elementary years do not understand many of the bible stories if they are read directly from the text. The vocabulary, the language structure, even the brevity of some of the stories are geared to adult ears. Children need more detail, repetition and, in many cases, adapted vocabulary. Young students are better taught

bible stories through children's versions of the scriptures such as *Little People's Paperbacks* and *Arch Books*. Many of the so-called children's Bibles, it must be noted, are not geared to early childhood levels. Editors frequently think that the addition of illustrations makes a children's text usable, but illustrations alone won't always illuminate or explain the concept or vocabulary.

Children are best introduced to the Bible with activities appropriate for their level of learning—dramatizations, illustrations, retold stories, puppets, filmstrips and the like. Vocabulary must also be introduced according to the level of the students.

At each level of growth the teacher-catechist's work is to prepare students to grow in understanding. As with all study, learning occurs best when the appropriate learning level is recognized and utilized.

The word of God is received into human minds, ears and hearts according to the ability of the receivers. It is important, then, for teachers to reject the idea that the Bible can overcome all human obstacles such as age and immaturity and affect the lives of the hearers.

Ronald Goldman, author of *Readiness for Religion: A Basis for Developmental Religious Education* (Seabury Press), writes:

> The Bible is not a book for the young, but when placed alongside life in a relevant context, it may challenge, clarify and strengthen personal convictions in them. . . . If used too soon and irrelevantly, it may retard religious thinking and create negative attitudes and be a disservice to religious teaching.

In practice, junior high school students are ready and should have their own copies of the New Testament. A good paperback edition in which they can make notes or write their thoughts is best. High school students and adults need the Old and New Testaments in editions that are readable and affordable, and, for most times, portable.

The American Bible Society (P.O. Box 5677, Grand Central Station, New York, New York 10163) offers very inexpensive scripture selections to give to children for various occasions. For a few cents each, the Christmas story with illustrations or "Jesus Blesses the Little Children" can be given to each child. This non-profit organization also offers special education selections, signed English scriptures for those with impaired hearing, and scriptures for the visually handicapped as well as some braille materials. They list Spanish materials in their catalog and information about materials in other languages is also available.

National Bible Week is an interfaith observance that is set to coincide with Thanksgiving in the United States. Information and materials may be obtained from the Laymen's National Bible Committee (815 Second Avenue, New York, N.Y. 10017). The Publication Office of the United States Catholic Conference (1312 Massachusetts Ave. N.W., Washington D.C. 20005) also lists promotional materials and resources for National Bible Week.

BUSY-WORK AND GIMMICKS

There are projects and activities that teach, enrich and develop; there are projects and activities that keep students busy, occupied and, hopefully, quiet. Each teacher has to learn to evaluate activities and projects with regard to the students' growth, not necessarily with regard to the teacher's peace and quiet.

When looking at material for projects and activities, or when planning work that keeps all the students occupied, teaching catechists must remember that everything should relate to the theme or main idea of that day. The teacher can't say, in looking over materials, "Hey, this is an excellent project, or puzzle or worksheet! How can I *make it fit in* with my lesson?" The theme must come first, and then the appropriate questions follow: Does this clarify the lesson, reinforce the theme or help the students remember? Will it be interesting and helpful to them or will it simply keep

them busy? Students always know the difference between enriching work and busy-work.

Of course teacher-catechists will want to avoid gimmicks—activities that are just too far-fetched to be considered seriously in catechetics. Using gimmicks or busy-work in religion classes not only causes the students to lose interest in the theme of the day, but actually changes the direction of the class itself. The focus of the class as a *religion* class may be lost by using poorly selected learning activities.

Here are some examples of busy-work gimmicks. These suggestions have all been published. Perhaps we need to be reminded that just because an idea is in print does not necessarily mean it is a good one. *Caveat emptor!* Let the buyer beware!

▶ How many words can you find in the word RESURRECTION? (This might be a good project for a language-arts class, but it has nothing to do with religion or religious education.)

▶ Help the three kings find their way out of the maze. (Substitute any biblical or church figure for the kings and you have an infinite number of mazes, all irrelevant to religious education.)

▶ Draw the other half of the elephant, one of the largest animals God has created.

▶ Draw faces on the prophets.

▶ Sew clothes for the statue of Mary.

▶ Have a baby shower for Mary.

▶ Give the kids paints and a piece of black paper. Now tell them to portray their souls to you.

▶ Do a magician's act, showing the miracles of Jesus.

It is obviously essential for the teacher-catechist to learn to evaluate learning activities wisely.

C

CATECHESIS

CATECHETICAL CENTER

Catechetical Directory
  (see *NATIONAL CATECHETICAL DIRECTORY*)

CATECHISM

CATECHIST

CATECHUMENATE

CELEBRATION

CERTIFICATION OF TEACHER-CATECHISTS

CHRISTMAS

CHURCH

CLASSROOM MANAGEMENT

Cognitive Psychology
  (see LEARNING THEORY)

COMMANDMENTS

COMMISSIONING OF CATECHISTS

COMMUNICATIONS

COMMUNITY

CONFIRMATION

CONFRATERNITY OF CHRISTIAN DOCTRINE (CCD)

CONTRACT LEARNING

Coordinator of Religious Education
  (see DIRECTOR OF RELIGIOUS EDUCATION)

CREATIVITY

CREED

CURRICULUM

When Jesus had finished these parables he left the district; and, coming to his home town, he taught the people in their synagogue in such a way that they were astonished and said, "Where did the man get this wisdom and these miraculous powers? This is the carpenter's son, surely?" (Mt 13:53-54).

C

CATECHESIS

Catechesis refers to efforts which help individuals and communities acquire and deepen Christian faith and identity through initiation rites, instruction, and formation of conscience. It includes both the message presented and the way in which it is presented (*NCD*, No. 5).

The bishops emphasize content and method and the continuous process of renewal for the individual and the community. They insist:

Catechesis is incomplete if it does not take into account the constant interplay between gospel teaching and human experience—individual and social, personal and institutional, sacred and secular (No. 35).

Catechesis is to be concerned with person and society, with commitment and service to the church and the world.

The use of the word *catechesis* is significant. The bishops have chosen a word used almost exclusively by the Catholic community, one that has its roots in the very early church. It derives from the Greek root meaning "to teach, to inform," and was applied to the process of instruction (to catechize) leading to commitment and to the period of formation (catechumenate) preceding full reception into the community. In St. Augustine's time the word had also taken on the idea "to resound, to echo, to sing out."

In these contexts, *catechesis* seems to have been chosen as the word that best describes the process that includes instruction but also goes beyond that meaning to commitment, action and involvement.

See also CATECHUMENATE.

CATECHETICAL CENTER

One of the most hopeful signs of a changing time has been the appearance of catechetical centers. The term covers a broad range, from space in diocesan educational offices to some classrooms in the parish school to buildings designed and set up exclusively for catechetical work.

Ideally, a catechetical center provides resources and facilities geared to the broad scope of catechesis. The center should include a library for all ages, office space for the DRE and for different programs, and multipurpose rooms for day and evening programs aimed at parishioners in all age groups.

In parishes that support a school the catechetical center may be housed in the school building. These "part-time" centers require resource rooms and office space so that the volunteer teachers, the aides and the secretarial help have adequate room for meetings, have access to materials for their classes, and can confer with the DRE.

On the diocesan level, catechetical centers should provide a rich source of materials and programs. If the diocese is large, one centrally located center may not conveniently serve all the parishes in the diocese. Regional centers should then be set up to provide easy access to the resources available through the diocese. Diocesan centers should have evening hours so that teacher-catechists who have other commitments during the standard working day can use the centers.

One novel idea that should be noted is the catechetical center in a shopping mall or airport. Usually located near a chapel, such centers provide shoppers and travelers with reading rooms, viewing areas, and scheduled conferences and lectures. Catechetical centers, especially in the malls, may be the way to meet the people where they are.

CATECHISM

For years the word most associated with all types of religious education programs was *catechism*. "Did you go to catechism class?" "What did you get for catechism?" The single word epitomized the method, the content and the tradition. In the United States, of course, the *Baltimore Catechism* dominated American catechetics from 1884 up to the early 1960s. It wasn't the only text, but it was to American

Catholic religious education what the McGuffey readers had been to American public-school education.

The question-and-answer method was characteristic of the catechism. The book presented in orderly and precise language a compendium of faith and its practice meant to be absorbed for a lifetime. In practice, educators taught catechists how to teach the catechism, and students were expected to memorize and absorb the content.

The weakness of these texts was in the sequencing of topics and the language used. They did not start where the learner was, nor did they consider the students' background, language and experiences. They followed a sequence of belief logical for adults. The authors of the *Baltimore Catechism* (Numbers One, Two and Three) attempted to keep the same sequence and basic vocabulary, with some limited consideration for the young, and some added material for older students.

Vatican II, with its shift in theological and pastoral thinking, freed us from the slavish use of catechisms and gave legitimacy to the work of many religious-education theorists of the 20th century. In today's catechetics the scope and sequence are geared to the learner, the language is appropriate, the role of memory has been reconsidered and the format has been changed.

See also TEXTBOOKS.

CATECHIST

The *NCD* uses the term *catechist* in a broad sense to designate anyone who formally or informally participates in the catechetical ministry. It does, however, qualify the term for more specific roles, for example, parents, teachers, principals in Catholic schools, parish catechists, coordinators or directors of religious education (DREs), personnel in the national or diocesan offices, deacons, priests and bishops.

We are using the *NCD* description of parish catechists:

> Parish catechists, many of whom are volunteers, may be engaged in catechizing adults, young people, children, or those with special needs . . . in a variety of teaching and learning programs, liturgical experiences, classes, retreats, service programs, study clubs, and similar activities (No. 213).

As we say in the Introduction, our concern is basically with the teacher-catechist, the front-line person who works in CCD programs, or perhaps is a full or part-time religion teacher in the Catholic school system.

CATECHUMENATE

In contemporary American catechetics there is a movement to direct more of our efforts and expenditures to the adult community.

With this move toward adult learning, the revival of the catechumenate has been of considerable significance to some educators and should be noted by all catechists, whether directly involved in adult work or not. A 1966 decree from the Second Vatican Council called for the adult rites of initiation—baptism, Eucharist and confirmation—to be revised and restored to the catechumenate.

The *General Catechetical Directory* (1971) describes the catechumenate for adults as follows:

> The catechumenate for adults, which at one and the same time includes catechesis, liturgical participation, and community living is an excellent example of an institute that springs from the cooperation of diverse pastoral functions. Its purpose is to direct the spiritual journey of persons who are preparing themselves for the reception of baptism, and to give directions to their habits of thoughts and changes in moral living. It is a preparatory school in Christian living, an introduction to the religious, liturgical, charitable and apostolic life of the People of God (No. 130).

From this revised catechumenate and the work on the sacraments came the *Rite of Christian Initiation of Adults*, a marvelous document through which catechists can learn much more about the meaning of the sacraments of baptism, Eucharist and confirmation and how they are to be viewed in an adult context.

An understanding of the church's idea of the adult life of faith is seen in the passages through which an adult generally proceeds: stages of evangelization, catechumenate, purification, and enlightenment and post-baptismal catechesis. What adult religious education means in this context is continuous growth and exploration.

In some parish programs the *Rite of Christian Initiation of Adults* is used not only for those in the catechumenate, but in the faith formation of adults who are already Catholics and want to be renewed.

CELEBRATION

A celebration is a *wonderful* thing; it is a time to go beyond ourselves, to sing, to dance, to cry, to feast, to forgive, and to forget. And what do people celebrate? They celebrate the things, events and people too great to be contained in everyday life—birth, death, love, heroic leaders, saints and God.

Celebrations help us to remember, be proud, be aware of what it is to be human, and to reach out to the divine. They are days of paradox because we touch the untouchable; we "dream the impossible dream"; we are replenished and exhausted, and not always fully renewed. Our expectations of celebrations sometimes exceed our grasp. These are the days of remembrance and hope.

Catechists are called both to celebrate and to teach celebration. In the celebration of the sacraments, we bring alive acts of Christ in the birth and death cycle of human beings and the world. Throughout the year we celebrate events such as Christ's birth, death and resurrection and call them our holy days. In all this there is something so human that it is found in every place and time.

Each people has its own ways of celebrating itself. As Christian teachers we need to be aware of our history and hopes. From this awareness teachers can help students understand and join in the celebrations of the Christian community. Without it we lose touch with those parts of existence that give us life and meaning.

For a simple example of celebration, there is the Judaeo-Christian sabbath. We work for six days and are required to take a holy day, to move away from working with creation to reflect on the Creator and creation, and from this to be renewed and refreshed. Celebration begins as we learn to stop, to take time, to reflect and to play.

We teach celebration mostly by celebrating experiences shared by our students and ourselves in the parish community. Teachers and leaders help young people, at each level of growth, come to a greater understanding of a holy day. The rituals of birth, marriage, death and forgiveness, and the liturgies for holy days become more meaningful as the community itself celebrates.

Since Vatican II there has been a renewed effort to help the community understand who and what it is through its festivities and celebrations. Each person has to be prepared to join into the community life. Catechetical renewal includes a rediscovery of our feasts, and a refreshening and a reshaping of our rituals to make this possible.

Of course, celebration does not begin in the classroom, but it is one place where young children especially learn that to be Christian is to be a celebrant and to be in wonder. And from learning activities that include feasts and festivals, liturgies and paraliturgies, hopefully children will move more easily into a community of celebrants. What much of this book is about is the development of programs, at all levels, that reflect the call of the church to renew the celebration of Christian life in the world today.

See also LITURGY, PARALITURGY and HOLY DAYS AND HOLIDAYS.

CERTIFICATION OF TEACHER-CATECHISTS

Among the problems of catechetical programs is, Who shall teach? Who is qualified? Who decides? How can diocesan standards be enforced? The *NCD* suggests that diocesan offices

establish norms for accrediting catechists, including directors and coordinators, catechists in parish programs, Catholic school personnel, etc. These norms should require demonstrated competence and should not be based solely on "paper credentials" (No. 218).

Most dioceses have established teacher-training programs with specific requirements for courses in doctrine, scripture, liturgy and educational methodology and psychology. Upon completion, a certificate is given to the individual and notice given to the diocesan offices and the parish. Some dioceses have formal ceremonies for the newly certified teacher-catechists, and special recognition is given for advanced work.

In theory the process of certification assures certain standards and provides DREs with trained teachers. It is also extremely helpful for screening unsuitable candidates *before* they get to the classroom or, in some instances, for helping poorly prepared but dedicated teachers get needed help.

In practice there has been a pull between the need for teacher-catechists and the desire to upgrade the quality of teaching. *The National Inventory for Catechetical Programs* (United States Catholic Conference) indicates that parishes are still filling teacher-catechist positions with untrained people and that not enough parishes have teacher-training certification programs available.

See also TEACHER PREPARATION AND TRAINING.

CHRISTMAS

The commercial aspects of Christmas end with the last sale on Christmas Eve or perhaps at the gift exchange the day after Christmas. From that point on, the merchants are concerned about the next sales surge—Valentine's Day in February.

For teacher-catechists, however, Christmas is the beginning of a season, a time to celebrate the many manifestations of Christ. Lessons after Christmas should continue the theme with stories of the epiphany, the baptism of the Lord, the call of the apostles, the wedding at Cana and the presentation in the Temple. This is the time to give birth to ideas about hope, joy, love; it is the time to talk with students about Jesus being born into our lives. It is a period to focus on Christ, the Emmanuel, the fulfillment of the prophecies brought to us in the readings and lessons of Advent.

Unfortunately, some teacher-catechists focus their energies on Christmas day and a tiny baby; lessons in January make Christmas look like a distant past event. Of course, to know Jesus is to know about his birth and his parents, and we *begin* with that event. But catechesis doesn't end with the historical commemoration of the manger in Bethlehem. We celebrate Christ's birthday not to bring back the image of a baby, but to bring to mind the person and the new beginnings.

Religious education programs generally cancel classes during the big feasts of Easter and Christmas so students can celebrate these feasts with their parents or within the larger parish community. Unfortunately, many children never get to celebrate the feast of Christmas, and the last word about Jesus comes with the last religion class in Advent.

Catechetical programs need to consider some ways that the Advent preparation for Christmas is not lost when we actually get to the 25th of December and the weeks after. It might be helpful to have a party or liturgy during the Christmas vacation instead of during the last religion class before Christmas. Christmas decorations, displays and bulletins should be used throughout January.

Catechetical teamwork is needed to make Christmas meaningful for students. The DRE, along with the parish liturgical committee, needs to incorporate young people into the liturgies of Christmas.

Home activities are important, and suggestions can be sent home with the students. The basic idea is to avoid a gap between the Advent preparation with its many class activities and the possible emptiness of the feast itself in the home or parish celebrations.

Christmas has become little more than a winter holiday for many people. Teacher-catechists need to join with each member of the faith community in keeping the birth of

Jesus and his continued presence in the world as the real message of this joyful and peaceful holy day.

See also ADVENT and HOLY DAYS AND HOLIDAYS.

CHURCH

Good teachers work from their own positive experiences to help students learn. Teacher-catechists should think about how they came to be a part of the church, real members of the family. Invariably the first steps were acceptance and knowledge and comfortableness in a certain group of people, in a certain place.

This very human approach was also the way of Jesus and the biblical writers. Jesus knew people; he called them by name. He asked his listeners to rest, to be comfortable; he wanted his disciples to take care of his hearers' needs. He took children close to him and spoke with them.

If children are to experience and to understand church as the people of God, as community, they need to see and know the people at the altar, in the choir loft, next to them in the pew. They have to know what's special about the house of God and be familiar with their community's buildings—convents, rectories, schools and parish centers. Children need help in understanding that the people are the church.

Many students know very little about people and places we group under the word *church*. In an informal study of elementary-grade students, we were surprised to find out how little they knew about who's who and what's where. Most youngsters knew their teacher's name, the room they were assigned to and where the nearest water fountain and lavatory were. A few of them knew the principal and the parish priest connected with the program. A small minority could give the pastor's name, tell where the convent was, what the rectory was for, and what a lector did at Mass.

All these little bits of knowledge are only the beginning of being at home in the parish community. Introductions into the small groups that make up the larger community help students feel like a part of the group that we call *church*. Tours of the religious-education office, the sacristy, the choir loft, the parish meeting room, the sanctuary and the school help them understand the various functions of parish.

Meeting people in the parish who serve in various roles—pastor and associates, sisters and brothers, sacristans, secretaries, DRE, custodian, eucharistic ministers, permanent deacons, representatives of parish service organizations—is an important beginning for students learning about church.

For all students, starting with their own experience of church in their community prepares them for a greater understanding of the whole church. It is in coming to know, to recognize, to say hello to this living church that students begin to see and understand the great concept of the church as *people of God* as well as the place these people come together.

See also COMMUNITY.

CLASSROOM MANAGEMENT

Orderly procedures are essential to any efficient group operation. Classroom management, sometimes called "housekeeping," includes many activities such as attendance taking, record keeping and book distribution that contribute to the general orderliness and efficiency of the classroom. As a general rule, the better the group is managed, the fewer discipline problems will occur.

Getting a group in and out of a room, finding seats, hanging up outer clothing, checking on absentees are all procedures that have to be worked out in advance so they take a minimum of time away from the exploration of ideas. Be sure that students, teachers, administrators, substitutes and parents all are informed of the procedures that are decided upon. Here are some areas to cover in planning sessions:

▶ Establish times and appropriate signals for arrival, beginning of classes, completion of classes and dismissal. Students and adults need the security of regular schedules. Deviation from the schedule by one group can be disruptive to everyone in the program.

▶ Decide on attendance record procedures. Consider using aides to record attendance and placing the sheet in a manila envelope attached by a rubber band to the doorknob outside the classroom. Administrative aides can collect the sheets without interrupting the lesson.

▶ Use aides, if possible, to help prepare and distribute books and other materials. Have the materials set out in advance.

▶ Plan time for use of bathroom facilities, especially if students are coming from another school for an after-school program. Also establish a general policy for bathroom use during class time. Hall aides or monitors are helpful, especially with the younger grades.

▶ Establish a standard procedure for absentees. Some parishes call the home; others rely on postcards or letters. Good communication between program and parents provides a check on truants and is a safety precaution.

Plan for emergencies. If a child gets sick during class, use common sense. Sometimes resting or getting a drink of water is all that the situation requires. In more serious situations the students should be accompanied to the office by an aide or another student and the parents contacted. *Someone should remain with the child until parents or guardians arrive.* Some emergencies demand that medical assistance be called immediately and the parents notified.

Some procedures within the classrooms will vary depending on the teacher. These details still need to be planned in advance:

▶ Decide whether to take attendance by the roll-call method or by seating plan. Within the first few weeks, the teacher should know all the students by name. Continued or delayed attendance taking is distracting to the class and takes up valuable time.

▶ Establish a suitable and effective seating arrangement. One method is to allow students to choose their own seats and insist that each

person keep that seat until everyone in the class knows everyone else. Another method is to use a seating plan. Alphabetizing is certainly easy, but it is probably not the most effective method of building community.

▶ Allow time and plan the procedure for collecting materials after lessons. It is not good group management to yell after students to return books as they leave the room.

▶ Establish procedures for distributing, sharing and collecting art materials and other supplies. Be very specific on the use of scissors, staples and other sharp items. Plan to have assistance when you are involved in projects if it is at all possible. (Don't avoid projects because they're messy. Just make careful plans!)

▶ Decide which classroom chores can be the students' responsibility. Assign these chores on a rotating basis.

See also DISCIPLINE IN THE CLASSROOM and EMERGENCIES AND FIRST AID.

COMMANDMENTS

The Ten Commandments are basically a *summary* statement of the richness and complexity of people's relationship to the Creator and to each other. The commandments are rooted in history: "Of old, the divine pattern for human experience was set forth in the decalogue" (*NCD*, No. 100). In Jesus' new covenant, he affirms the decalogue and summarizes it in the two great commandments of love of God and love of neighbor.

The *NCD* places the commandments within the broader context of Jesus' teaching. "The specifics of morality should be taught in the light of the Ten Commandments, the Sermon on the Mount, especially the beatitudes and Christ's discourse at the Last Supper" (No. 105).

The present approach eliminates the slavish memorization of the commandments at too early an age, and insists that morality not be confined to ten statements. And while the *NCD* urges that "students should know the decalogue as part of their religious heritage"

(No. 100), moral development rather than "keeping the commandments" is the main thrust. This development begins as early as a child is capable of understanding but, as has been stressed continuously in the *NCD*, with language and content appropriate to the child's level of learning.

A question frequently asked, "Aren't they teaching the commandments any more?" is unrealistic and inaccurate in terms of what the *NCD* suggests and most religion programs include in their course of study. Children are taught what God has revealed in the many sources of revelation but the approach is to help children understand God's word, law and love at their level. A second-grade student, for example, has little or no concept of the sixth commandment. For some, adultery means to disobey an adult. As children mature, the commandments are studied along with other equally important moral statements as guides and tools for making decisions in today's world.

See also BEATITUDES, MORALITY, MORAL DEVELOPMENT, SIN and RECONCILIATION.

COMMISSIONING OF CATECHISTS

A very positive sign that catechists are achieving a rightful place in the ministry of the church has been the commissioning ceremony suggested and recommended by the *NCD*. As early as 1956 the idea of a commissioning ceremony was officially requested, at the First International Congress of Pastoral Liturgy held at Assisi.

At this congress one bishop strongly suggested that anyone in a permanent ministerial position in the church community must have the formal, personal commission of the church, the special ordination that goes with the position.

Commissioning a person for a service is, of course, not new to the church. Remember all the minor orders that existed—porter, acolyte, lector and exorcist? These minor orders lost their individual identities through absorption

into the priesthood. Now, however, with the restored concept of ministry shared among the larger community, there is hope that formal commissioning will be developed into an official liturgical ceremony presided over by the bishop or a delegate.

At present there are many ceremonies commissioning or installing teacher-catechists after their training is completed. Many parishes hold this celebration on Catechetical Sunday which is at the end of September, near the beginning of religion classes. One example of such a program is the covenant ceremony in which the teacher-catechists pledge service to the community. The pledge is received by the pastor in the name of Jesus Christ and the community.

COMMUNICATIONS

There is a very practical aspect of communication that needs to be noted: the communication of information, schedules, decisions, programs and all those messages that keep groups moving and individuals in touch. These communiques take many forms. Here are the most pertinent to teacher-catechists:

Staff Notes. These are essential for every program, and especially for part-time programs with teachers coming and going on different schedules and/or classes in homes or several buildings. Since hopefully the notes get to everyone on the staff, their use cuts down on forgetfulness and misunderstood verbal messages. The notes should include announcements of workshops, courses, meetings, deadlines, and staff news; seasonal ideas and items; pedagogical tips; reviews or announcements of any new materials in religious education; meditation material for the staff; health and safety reminders; and rules and directions for record keeping. Notes can be delivered to the teacher-catechists in their classrooms each week or, if classes are held in homes, they can be picked up after Sunday Mass at a designated place.

Parish Bulletin. Many parish bulletins are setting aside a section for religious education news and announcements. This is also a good way of insuring some coordination of activities and themes among parish groups.

Calendar. Teachers should receive calendars at the beginning of the school year with all the major dates for the coming year. This helps teachers and parents plan their family lives with less confusion. Holidays, sacramental celebration schedules, meeting days, and other special activities that need long-range planning should be marked on this calendar.

Messages to Parents. Parents need to be kept informed about all aspects of the program. They should receive a calendar of dates important to them and their children. Letters and memos sent throughout the year are helpful in keeping parents posted about changes in the calendar, in calling attention to special events, or in requesting help. For important messages, mailing is safer than sending notes home with the students.

Newspapers. News releases to Catholic and secular newspapers provide a wide reach for announcements of programs and activities. Pictures of group projects and activities are also accepted by newspapers.

Television. Many local cable stations now provide free community bulletin board service. Investigate how your religious education program can use this service.

Telephone Chains. Sometimes a class has to be cancelled, or even an entire program called off, and there isn't enough time to send notices. It's too impractical for one person to call every student or teacher. A telephone chain arranged at the beginning of the year may be the only practical way to reach people. Several chains may be needed. Each teacher should have one worked out with the parents; and DREs and grade-level coordinators should be able to reach teacher-catechists. A chain works by having a message relayed by phone to several people, each of whom contacts several other people, and so on.

See also HANDBOOKS.

COMMUNITY

Jesus' words, "By this love you have for one another, everyone will know that you are my disciples" (Jn 13:35) call for catechetical programs that show not only knowledge acquired, but life and love shared.

Much of the criticism of some former catechetical theories and practices was directed toward the intellectualism, the stress on memory, and the rewards for perfect attendance and high test scores. Catechetics became *proficiency* in religious knowledge with *perfect performance* at the reception of the sacraments. The emphasis on memory and ritual behavior often left little time for sharing the good news in action with signs and experiences of community, with communal service.

Community and service are critical to catechesis. The *NCD* lists "the four interrelated purposes of catechesis: to proclaim the mysteries of faith; to foster community; to encourage worship and prayer; to motivate service to others" (No. 227). In another passage the *NCD* states, "Authentic experience of Christian community leads one to the service of others" (No. 210).

We teach what we know. Teacher-catechists who are involved in fostering community also need to experience it. Community is formed in a variety of ways. The *NCD* suggests ways to foster community that apply to both students and teachers: "Beginning with acceptance of individual strengths and weaknesses, it progresses to relationships based on shared goals and values. It grows through discussions, recreation, cooperation on projects, and the like" (No. 209).

Some specific ways to promote community for students and faculty include:

▸ providing opportunities for teacher-catechists to share time together, to talk about their ideas over a cup of coffee.

▸ organizing teacher get-togethers, not only faculty meetings and planning sessions, but social programs that include spouses or dates.

▸ promoting grade-level activities that afford opportunities for students to share experiences with others besides their classmates.

▶ arranging for the whole student body to share in a liturgy several times during the course of a school year.

▶ inviting upper grade students to assist the primary students in certain activities.

▶ involving parents in as many activities as possible; helping them share in the experience of their child's group.

▶ offering family get-togethers for the religious education program.

▶ planning joint activities for the students of the parish school and the students in the CCD programs.

▶ introducing new teachers to the staff and placing them with more experienced teachers.

▶ encouraging participation in workshops, congresses and institutes which not only assist teachers in their work, but help people come and grow together.

▶ helping staff prepare workshops and programs for some neighboring parishes. Working together and sharing ideas while reaching out to others builds community.

▶ encouraging cooperation and participation in community and parish service projects.

Each group has its own lists of what brings life and community, but lists do not have lives of their own. The staff gives life. And community begins with each active participant.

See also SERVICE.

CONFIRMATION

Confirmation is viewed as completing the sacramental initiation, but that does not mean it should be the conclusion of active catechetical life. Attendance in catechetical programs after the reception of confirmation takes a precipitous drop, and it is rightfully a cause of concern that our confirmation preparation doesn't succeed in opening up students to future study and further growth in our junior and senior high school programs.

Confirmation asks for a commitment on the part of the young Christian. Increasingly, the emphasis is on a preparation that involves the idea of acceptance of the role of a mature person in a community dedicated to service. As a result, in practice, the age for the reception of confirmation has shifted. Customarily the sacrament was received about the ages of 10 or 12. Now, more commonly, the students are 12, 14, or in some dioceses, 17 or older.

The type of preparation has changed accordingly. The NCD, after noting that activities are always appropriate to the age level, speaks now of "performance standards for Church membership and community service; requiring a specified minimum number of hours of service to qualify for Confirmation; a letter of request for Confirmation; formational programs of catechesis extending over two or three years; and the use of adult advisors" (No. 119). It is fascinating to see the idea of performance standards after so many years where the norms for confirmation reception were generally academic memorization and suitable classroom behavior.

The new preparations obviously require a change in youth ministry and the junior and senior high school curricula on confirmation. The very idea of confirmation as sharing in the adult life of the community now involves "the parish community which has an obligation to participate in the catechetical preparation of those to be confirmed." The new forms of service and performance require different structures. No longer is the curriculum design for confirmation centered on classroom lectures or discussions; rather adult advisors and parents need to be part of the program which helps these adolescents learn to serve and also aids them in their decision making.

Many parishes have developed new plans for confirmation and are utilizing specially trained youth ministers. The immediate preparation for the sacrament may include a retreat day or weekend. Candidates for the sacrament are interviewed by the DRE or the priest for a more personal contact with the student and for a better understanding of what the youngster perceives. Although a whole group is prepared for the reception of this sacrament, each student is made aware that he or she must make a personal decision to be

CONTRACT LEARNING   45

confirmed. (And the community, including the parents, must respect the right of a student to delay or even refuse the sacrament.)

The shift in the confirmation programs from passive to active participation on the part of students requires a major retooling of catechetical efforts at the junior and senior high school levels. The work of youth ministers, the increasing emphasis on service and community, and the development of curriculum materials are aids for teacher-catechists whose work is in this area.

CONFRATERNITY OF CHRISTIAN DOCTRINE (CCD)

The expression *CCD* has become a familiar shorthand term for the Confraternity of Christian Doctrine, a worldwide catechetical organization whose primary goal has been the teaching apostolate. Although its origins go back to St. Charles Borromeo in the 16th century, the movement in the United States began in New York in 1902. It achieved nationwide recognition and organization in 1935 under the impetus of Bishop O'Hara, and its form and function dominated American catechetics up to the '70s.

The parish structure of the CCD was headed by the priest-director who met with and worked through the executive board of officers and division chairmen (teachers, fishers, helpers, discussion clubs, parent-educators and apostles of good will). All members of the confraternity program had a role in the proclamation of the Christian message.

The structure of the CCD has changed in our time, but the name has stayed with us. In many parishes CCD has become a generic term for religious education outside the Catholic school. The following dialogue is still symptomatic of CCD in many parishes with Catholic schools.

"Who's the boy with John?"

"Oh, he's a CCD kid."

"A what kind of kid?"

"I dunno—he goes to public school."

Catechist magazine took a reader survey about the use of the term CCD. It found a small number of parishes retaining the name CCD meaning Confraternity of Christian Doctrine; others were using the initials to stand for something more meaningful to them such as "Continuing Christian Doctrine," or "Christ-Centered Development." Some programs chose not to use CCD at all and developed another acronym, PREP, to describe their "Parish Religious Education Program"; others simply chose "RE" for "Religious Education."

Our own informal survey has shown that catechetical programs are called religion classes, religion school, bible school, Sunday school, released time and, for many still, CCD. The lack of a common expression indicates some loss of the strong identity of the past associated with the concept of CCD.

CONTRACT LEARNING

Contract learning is an attempt to meet the individual needs and interests of students by establishing a contract between the student and teacher. The student agrees to complete a certain task, perform a service, or research a question within a set period of time for an agreed amount of credit or acknowledgment.

The contract helps the teacher individualize learning, in a structured way, for students with widely divergent backgrounds, different rates of learning and different levels of maturity.

This technique requires much advance work on the part of the teacher and more planning time and conference hours. It is perhaps most valuable and practical with junior and senior high school students who may be ready for this type of independent study, and who may see it as a challenging elective. It could be helpful where attendance problems at the adolescent age level reveal some strong need for innovation or challenge. Contracts can also be used in specific preparation for the reception of confirmation.

Contracts are an example of individualization, which has its roots in sound educational principles. It allows for individual growth, the interests of the student and some freedom from routine group work.

The student and teaching catechist meet to discuss the terms of the contract. An agreement might be to study a particular topic with a specific type of report due. Or it can be a creative project such as planning a liturgy, an art project or a community celebration. In another area, it can be a service to be performed for an individual or institution.

At the initial meeting, practical arrangements must be worked out: What type of assistance will the student need? Are any permissions required? Will the student be working with someone else? What is a practical work schedule? When will the next meeting be held? What is expected to be accomplished by that meeting?

When the actual terms of the agreement are worked out, the contract is written and signed by the teacher-catechist and the student. The teacher agrees to assist and support, and to provide acknowledgment of the completed project; for example, a grade, an announcement in the bulletin, a certificate for the completion of confirmation preparation. Or the student may simply seek the satisfaction of work well done. The student agrees to a specific task and a date due.

In one parish, junior high school students volunteered to work on a one-to-one basis with the teaching catechists in lieu of regularly scheduled classes. They worked out contracts at the beginning of the semester and met with teachers for assistance and when encouragement was needed. Students chose two of the following three areas for their work: research, liturgy or service. Each student was also involved in a social contract where everyone worked together. This provided the social interaction so valuable in youth ministry.

A significant feature of contract learning is its flexibility. It provides for individual needs which cannot always be met with traditional methods.

CREATIVITY

Some words paraphrased from William James, the psychologist, will be helpful. He said we all possess the capacity to become creative but learn to be uncreative. He blamed parents and teachers who taught children not to think but to accept.

Creativity is not a special gift for the few, but a human characteristic that is common to all. Our concept of creativity cannot be the stereotypical picture of a painter or musician who comes up with a brilliantly different approach to music or art. A person who can look at a problem, a question or a new situation, and see the many ways it is possible to solve, discover or explore it, shows creativity.

Teacher-catechists who want to offer opportunities for students to grow in creativity provide an atmosphere that encourages thinking and acting among the students. They assist students in employing divergent thinking, that is, thinking that helps students see different aspects of an idea, that helps them be open to more than one solution, that helps them explore away from and beyond the regular paths. This approach encourages originality and innovation. It should be noted that much of the thought of Jesus would be categorized as divergent thinking.

Where does creativity fit into religious education programs, particularly those designed for the study of norms and traditions? Religious educators today find a real need to help young people develop facility in divergent thinking, especially in the area of morality. Discussing and eliciting creative responses to moral dilemmas in today's society is essential in assisting students in their intellectual, moral and personal growth.

On the level of *creative expression*, allowing the use of other forms of learning, such as art, music and drama, is critical to successful religious education programs. It is important to develop a climate for creativity: a sense of wonder and amazement at people's ability to learn, to create and to recreate the world around them; and the conviction that each person is called to share in creation.

CREED

For many of us the repetition of certain prayers, statements and pledges has been a part of our lives. We all know the Pledge of Allegiance, the national anthem and the Apostles' Creed. Perhaps some of us have occasionally said that we are too mechanical and don't think enough about what we are saying. There was a period in the United States in the 1960s when many students and adults wanted to reject anything that had been handed on in "rote" fashion and sought to talk only about what was truly "meaningful," "relevant" and "now."

The use of formulas, of words preserved and handed down from other generations, of traditional statements, is common to all—and for a good reason. It helps each generation hand on in a very simple but profound way its beliefs about itself and its reason for being. Creeds are in this category.

The creeds are sources of truth and statements to be taught, words that teacher-catechists must help the young learn and understand. Today the way creeds are introduced to young children is different. For the most part the memorization of the Apostles' Creed as a requirement for first communion is a thing of the past. But the presentation of the creed as a formula to be received into the mind, even if incompletely understood, and as a formula to be prayed in the liturgy, is certainly a task of the teacher.

The creeds are statements to grow up with, not too dissimilar to learning the opening words of the Declaration of Independence or the Pledge of Allegiance. Students learn to think about what they have heard and, from that, pursue its meaning. This is one of the ways we receive the truths and traditions that hopefully will be a part of our lives.

It is interesting to note that creeds have developed over the centuries, each formulated to fit a new insight or challenge to the faith. In 1969 Pope Paul VI issued a creed, a profession of faith, that is an indication of the formulation of the 20th century. In liturgical use, however, the Nicene Creed is the most common. The Apostles' Creed is recommended for use in liturgies for children since it is part of their catechetical formation and they are most familiar with it.

See also MEMORIZATION and PRAYER.

CURRICULUM

The word *curriculum* presents a great challenge to religious educators because it covers the questions of what should be taught and in what sequence. *Curriculum* derives from Latin meaning "the course to be run," a good choice because it indicates a certain limited area to be covered, not an aimless wandering around.

As would be expected, the *NCD* hopes that diocesan offices recommend curricula and textbooks and that "curricula . . . be properly sequenced, presenting essential truths in a manner appropriate to the abilities of the age group" (No. 229). Most publishers have taken seriously the directions of the *Directory* in preparing texts, working with catechetical and educational consultants, and seeking to obtain recommendations for use in the many dioceses.

One of the most significant statements in the *NCD* about curriculum is under the section on Catholic schools, but the principle given applies to all catechetical programs: "The school should have a set religion curriculum, with established goals and objectives, open to review and evaluation by parish boards and diocesan supervisory teams" (No. 232). It is obviously important that each school or religious education program decide what is important for its individual and particular needs, that the members of the parish as well as the diocese be consulted in planning the curriculum. A textbook series from a particular publisher should not determine the curriculum. Although the published works may have the approval or recommendation of the diocese, curriculum must be worked out by the parish and a textbook series chosen that reflects the needs of the students.

There is general consensus on the sequencing of curriculum material. The content and sequence for elementary schools are basically as follows:

First grade	God the Father, the Creator God's creation Introduction to Father, Son and Holy Spirit Me

Second grade	Getting to know Jesus
	Eucharist—basic preparation
	    for first communion
	Relationship with Jesus
	Some preparation for
	    reconciliation

Third grade	Jesus and his relationship to the community
Fourth grade	The Ten Commandments The beatitudes Christian conscience
Fifth grade	Church The seven sacraments
Sixth grade	Salvation history The Bible The Holy Spirit
Seventh grade	Confirmation New Testament Values
Eighth grade	History of the church Liturgy of the Eucharist Confirmation

High school curricula vary more, but most four-year programs center around a core of doctrine, liturgy, morality and Christology courses and also offer various electives.

Determining the curriculum for a parish, or for a diocese, is an ongoing process in which the development of new materials and the emergence of new issues and problems must be considered.

In the classroom, of course, each teacher-catechist needs to adapt the curriculum to the particular schedule, class, or even to a special student. This is a serious concern that needs special attention.

A common problem is having too few sessions for all the material that could be presented. Some teacher-catechists are comfortable selecting particular topics or special devotional materials; others are not. For the most part the DRE needs to be a supportive supervisor and coordinator who works with individual teacher-catechists and provides them with the skills and balance to make sound and practical classroom decisions.

See also MANUALS FOR TEACHERS and HANDBOOKS.

D

DANCE

Deaf
  (see HANDICAPPED)

DEATH EDUCATION

DEVELOPMENTAL PSYCHOLOGY

DEVELOPMENT OF DOCTRINE

DIARY

Diocesan Religious Education Offices
  (see CATECHETICAL CENTER)

DIRECTOR OF RELIGIOUS EDUCATION (DRE)

Directory
  (see *NATIONAL CATECHETICAL DIRECTORY*)

Disabled
  (see HANDICAPPED)

DISASTER DRILLS

DISCIPLINE IN THE CLASSROOM

DISCUSSION METHOD

DRE
  (see DIRECTOR OF RELIGIOUS EDUCATION)

DUPLICATING MATERIALS AND METHODS

DRAMA

When the festival was half over, Jesus went to the Temple and began to teach. The Jews were astonished and said, "How did he learn to read? He has not been taught." Jesus answered them:
   "My teaching is not from myself:
   it comes from the one who sent me;
   and if anyone is prepared to do his will,
   he will know whether my teaching is from God
   or whether my doctrine is my own" (Jn 7:14-17).

D

DANCE

One of the great biblical images is that of David dancing before the Ark of the Covenant, marvelous because it's so vibrant an image—a king "jumping for joy," for the sake of his God. "I am the Lord of the Dance!" We've not always, in our country and culture, grown used to religious movement. Some still think that the Shakers were strange. And although we delight in children's movement and applaud and encourage their dancing because it seems so free and spontaneous, we don't use it in religion classes.

Dance must be considered in its broadest meaning—motion characterized by rhythm, beat, some patterning that relates to music. Movements such as swaying, jumping, skipping, hopping and stepping are all part of dance. Children always combine rhythm and movement in their play. Watch a child jump rope in time with rhyme words or observe children playing "statues." Youngsters form parades, step in time, and learn to communicate with their feelings in the playfulness of the dance.

It would be helpful for teacher-catechists to think about the use of movement as a means of human expression, a way to express significant points in our lives, to celebrate, to take a stand, to communicate a belief, to hold up a value or to declare a human right. There are bridal processions and dances, military marches, civil rights and Holy Name parades, funeral processions and street festivals. People do not sit still for great moments or important feelings.

Catechetics needs to find a more prominent place for active movement in learning. For most teacher-catechists the simple use of motion activities, or play celebrations with dance during classes, will be the most helpful introduction for students.

At the junior and senior high school levels an understanding and appreciation of how dance is used in many countries and cultures to express religious sentiments of joy, sorrow, love and devotion could be an excellent elective or seminar for some students.

Some helpful resources for teacher-catechists:
Dance As Prayer (World Library Publications); *The Dance in Christianity* (Paulist Press); *The Spirit Moves: A Handbook of Dance and Prayer* (Liturgical Press).

See also PLAY and MUSIC.

DEATH EDUCATION

In recent years death and dying have become topics of concern in many areas of education. The moral questions connected with the dying who are kept alive by technological assistance, the decisions to be made by families of the critically ill, the psychological studies of the death process and its impact on the dying and the family, the special counseling for the dying and the survivors are all concerns of many teachers and counselors—and not only those connected with religious institutions.

Religious educators, of course, are involved in the subject of death and dying directly or indirectly. The death-resurrection theme is central to the Christian message and worship, and, of course, each member of the catechetical community, student or teacher, will be touched directly or communally by death experiences. The newer dimensions for teacher-catechists today are media presentations and discussions of the medical/technological questions of maintaining life or of defining when life begins or ends. Certainly teachers need to be aware of what is happening in this area and to incorporate this material into the curriculum.

On another point, Pierre Babin in two of his works, *Options* and *Methods*, calls for teachers to be alert to special times in students' lives and explore their meaning with students; for example, when a death occurs, it is then the "privileged moment" to talk about the meaning of death and dying.

Some media material is noted here to help teaching catechists.

The Butterfly Tree (Our Sunday Visitor) is a beautiful story for intermediate grades or to be read to younger children.

Good Night, Mrs. Foster (Ikonographics), a filmstrip that deals with death and dying, is good for middle grade children.

Death and Other Living Things (Pflaum/Standard) is a Christian Experience booklet for high school students and older.

DEVELOPMENTAL PSYCHOLOGY

Developmental psychology is that field of study which looks at the physical, emotional, intellectual and moral stages of human growth. The development of a personality is seen in terms of all these components. An understanding of developmental psychology will help teaching catechists choose methods and materials appropriate to the individual learner's stage of development.

A major chapter in the *NCD* is "Catechesis Toward Maturity in Faith" (Chapter VIII). It includes sections about the relationship between faith and human development and catechesis and human development.

> The Church encourages the use of the biological, social, and psychological sciences in pastoral care. . . . Manuals for catechists should take into account psychological and pedagogical insights, as well as suggestions about methods.
>
> The behavioral sciences cause neither faith nor growth in faith; but for that matter, neither does the catechist. . . .
>
> These sciences do, however, help us understand how people grow in their capacity for responding in faith to God's grace (No. 175).

The *NCD* outlines the following stages of human development: infancy and early childhood (birth to age 5); childhood (ages 6-10); preadolescence and puberty (10-13); adolescence; early adulthood; middle adulthood; and later adulthood.

Many contemporary educational psychologists have offered us insights into the developmental processes, and their works have both influenced and reinforced the thinking of religious educators working in the field. Here we provide in summary form the work of some key psychologists and educators who have been considered seriously by catechists.

Erik Erikson, a personality theorist, offers these stages of psychosocial development. Each stage typifies a crisis. Through the resolution of this crisis, a healthy personality emerges.

Erikson's Eight Ages of Man

Oral/Sensory	birth-1 year	basic trust *vs.* basic mistrust
Muscular/Anal	1-3 years	autonomy *vs.* shame
Locomotor/ Genital	3-6 years	initiative *vs.* guilt
Latency	6-12 years	mastery *vs.* inferiority
Puberty/ Adolescence	12-18 years	identity *vs.* role confusion
Young Adulthood	18-24 years	intimacy *vs.* isolation
Adulthood	24-60 years	generativity *vs.* stagnation
Maturity	60 years plus	ego integrity *vs.* despair

Jean Piaget, a Swiss psychologist, concentrates on cognitive development and points out that other areas of development relate and parallel cognitive thought. Children learn concepts only as they go through a series of developmental stages. These stages occur in sequence and are rooted in physical development.

Piaget's Stages of Cognitive Development

Sensory-Motor	birth-2 years	behavior dictated by the senses and motor activity
Pre-operational (intuitive)	2-7 years	develops ways of representing events and objects through symbols (including language)
Concrete Operations	7-11 years	beginning of some logical thought; solves problems in concrete terms
Formal Operations	11 and up	can abstract; can visualize logical solutions internally

Lawrence Kohlberg, an American, sees moral development occurring in a sequence with each stage qualitatively different from the next. There is a relationship between Piaget's system of cognitive development and Kohlberg's stages of moral development.

Kohlberg's Stages of Moral Growth

Basis of Judgment		Stages of Development
Pre-conventional (Pre-moral)	birth-9 (approx.)	1. Concern about self; "bad" is what is punished; "good" is what is rewarded
		2. Satisfaction of own needs; the needs of others considered only if it benefits self; reciprocal fairness
Conventional	9-15	3. "Good boy—nice girl" orientation; intentions become significant; motivation is "to be accepted"
		4. Authority, social order, maintenance of law and order are important
Post-conventional	15-adult (hopefully)	5. Social contract, legalistic orientation; personal rights; no legal absolutes
		6. Universal ethical principles; what is right is the decision of one's conscience based on ideas about rightness that apply to everyone

Ronald Goldman, an English educator-psychologist, discusses what he calls "readiness for religion" (also the name of one of his books). It is necessary to begin with the needs and experiences of children at their own level of development. There are developmental limits on what is taught based on the rate of natural growth and the life experiences of children and youth.

Goldman's Stages of a Child's Religious Thinking

Pre-religious (intuitive)	5-7 years	Confusion: God with parents, prayers based on material requests similar to requests to parents; bible stories relate the same magic and fantasy as fairy tales
Sub-religious (concrete operational)	7-9 years	Continued God/parent confusion; prayers unanswered because child did not pray right or God did not hear; Bible as literal
Personal Religious	9-12 years	God is supernatural, benevolent; prayer, altruistic but also for protection, self-improvement; likes ritual and formulated prayers; bad people do not have prayers answered; Bible is true, literal
Religious	13 and up	God can be related to abstract concepts; prayer is spiritual, gives sense of peace, communication; Bible, metaphorically and poetically true

James Fowler, an American professor of theology and human development, integrates the development of personality with religious and moral growth under what he describes as "faith development."

Fowler's Stages of Faith Development

0	Undifferentiated Faith	Prelinguistic; infants unconsciously form a disposition toward their world
I.	Intuitive-Projective Faith (3 to about 7)	Fantasy-filled; influenced by examples, moods, actions, and language of primal adults
II.	Mythical-Literal Faith	Children take on stories, beliefs and observances which symbolize belonging to their community; literal interpretations for beliefs, moral rules, and attitudes; symbols are one-dimensional and literal
III.	Synthetic-Conventional Faith	Experience extends beyond family; faith provides a coherent orientation in the midst of complex involvements, a synthesis of values and information and a unifying basis for identity and outlook
IV.	Individuative-Reflective Faith	Person must begin to take responsibility for commitments, lifestyle, beliefs and attitudes; individuality *vs.* being defined by the group; self-fulfillment *vs.* service to and being for others
V.	Paradoxical-Consolidative Faith (unusual before midlife)	Symbolic power reunited with conceptual meanings; reclaiming and reworking of one's past; critical recognition of one's social unconsciousness; can appreciate symbols, myths and rituals (own and others')
VI.	Universalizing Faith (rare)	Become incarnators and actualizers of the spirit of a fulfilled human community

DEVELOPMENT OF DOCTRINE

There is a phrase that gets little attention in catechetical manuals, and yet it is at the heart of many problems that some teachers face. It is *development of doctrine.* The *NCD* (No. 60) may be one of the few resources a teaching catechist reads that treat this question; it suggests that three aspects of development be noted: new and deeper insights into the meanings and application of doctrine can occur; new terminology can emerge for the expression of doctrine; and the church can define doctrines whose positions in tradition and revelation are not explicitly evident.

What might be most significant for teacher-catechists is the shift from a static, unchanging approach to faith and morals to a dynamic, living revelation. The *NCD* is saying to catechists that the notion that there is a body of truth, a book in an unchanging language somewhere that contains every truth we need to know now and forever, is not an accurate description of revelation and faith.

A corollary to the idea of development of doctrine is that the new perceptions and expressions of doctrine will ultimately be reflected in rituals and faith practices. As emphases shift, for example, from the passion and death of Jesus to the resurrection, the simple expression "funeral Mass for the dead" becomes the "Mass of resurrection for Christian burial." The Vatican Council's emphasis on the role of the church in the world today has led to new directions in Third-World theology.

For some teacher-catechists the concept of development is difficult in terms of certain other parts of the *NCD* that touch upon doctrinal content and methodology. In the very beginning of the document the authors write:

> Because catechesis is concerned with applying the certain, timeless teachings of faith to the uncertain, changing conditions of each generation, some errors of judgment, misplaced emphasis, and ill-timed innovations are likely. . . (No. 10).

The "certain" and "timeless" teachings, then, must be seen in the light of "new and deeper insights," and "new terminology." The document is stressing that the methods of catechesis today are so markedly different from many teachers' own experiences of religious education that there is some confusion as to what should be taught and how it is to be transmitted.

There are two problems: 1) change of material selected and the methodology, and 2) the complex long-range question of development of doctrine. Teacher-catechists need help for their own faith understanding and development, and for their students. The continued growth in theology and methodology becomes of paramount importance to all in the work of catechesis.

DIARY

"Of all the words of tongue and pen, the saddest are 'it might have been.' " These words have haunted most of us in our work, but we sometimes don't consider why our goals and hopes are not achieved. We lose track, we forget, we even put off what we want to do. An antidote to this problem is the diary or journal.

A diary is a tool teacher-catechists can use for self-evaluation. It can be a detailed account of the day's lesson, or just simple phrases in the margin of the teacher's manual, or a lesson plan which notes what did or did not happen.

One of the authors of this book kept a diary of his day-by-day experiences teaching a senior religion class. It was later published under the title *The Catechetical Experience* (Herder and Herder). The book evolved from his long-time habit as a teacher of reflecting in writing on classroom experiences, making notes after each class—of students' responses, his own preparations, the general direction of the group, and the possibilities of change. The diary was kept because it was too hard to remember (without notes) from month to month what *really* happened in each session.

The key to evaluating one's teaching is, of course, the willingness to be open to writing both successes and failures, to recording the difficulties, the actual exchanges and the disappointments.

From this process the teacher eventually can get a clearer view of what goes on in the actual classroom situation. Piveteau and Dillon in *Resurgence of Religious Education* (Religious Education Press) describe this author's diary experience as "not so much one of careful preparation and execution of a religion course as it was a continual reflection on the course of the course, questioning and changing as need arose from the process, procedures and teacher himself."

A diary can also be used by students. Many high-school and adult-education programs encourage the use of the diary or journal as an ongoing record of the reflections, thoughts, feelings and insights the learners are experiencing during the course. Depending upon the group processes and decisions the journal may be completely private or shared with the group on some occasions.

Diaries have a long history in the human reflective process. Their value is not in promoting self-praise or vanity, but in facilitating the type of self-examination that helps our work or our lives with others. In writing about our work we assume a type of responsibility for our behavior; we set down a record on which we measure ourselves.

See also LESSON PLANS and MANU-ALS FOR TEACHERS.

DIRECTOR OF RELIGIOUS EDUCATION (DRE)

Some words in the church have a tried and true ring about them. We're comfortable with them because they've been around so long and everyone knows what they mean, for example, *Father* Harvey, *Sister* Michele. We know the *pastor*, the *curate*, the *assistant*. But what is a *director of religious education* doing in our church? In fact, what is a DRE?

DREs are new, for us, in name and practice (and in some places do not even exist yet). How and why did we get this new job when everything was going so well? We had done without this person for several hundred years, at least.

Actually the job has always been with us. Someone was always responsible for sacramen-

tal preparation, for CCD classes, for Sunday schools. Frequently the youngest or newest priest in the rectory was in charge, with the actual operation under the direction of Sister Superior or her delegate. In some parishes, however, there were sisters who were specialists in religious education, such as the Mission Helpers of the Sacred Heart or the Glenmary Sisters. They would run a program until a regular parochial school was set up.

Somewhere along the way a change occurred. The CCD model, up to the 1960s, had a priest in charge of all religious instruction with a volunteer lay board. In the '50s, however, there was a germ of an idea that finally emerged into our present concept of religious education specialists. There were, at that time, theologians and catechists who were looking for and devising programs that would provide more theological preparation for catechists, and more pastoral and catechetical preparation for theologians and seminarians. At such centers as Catholic University of America new pastoral programs in the field of theology and education began to emerge. Catechetics, long a minor study for seminarians and priests, began to achieve some recognition in major seminaries and theological centers.

As more scholars and educators looked at the work of teaching religion, more became convinced that the catechetical field could not be left to the dedicated religious or priest who may or may not have had special training. Both in theory and practice it became evident that the training of religion teachers had to become separate and specialized. But if teachers with special preparation were needed, so too were directors who understood the new field, and also knew what programs and structures would be needed.

By the mid-to-late '60s there was an extraordinary growth in the number of graduate and professional programs for training in religious education. Out of this time came this new person, now most commonly called the director of religious education or DRE. Other terms have been used, such as *coordinator* or *minister of religious education*, but in the advertisements for jobs, *DRE* is most commonly used, and there is now a National Conference of Diocesan Directors of Religious Education which also uses the term *DRE* for local parish leaders.

The job description, as indicated from a 1980 conference on DREs, covers the following areas: catechist formation, recruitment, evaluation and continual supervision; ex officio member of an education committee or board in full charge of catechetical programs (the DRE generally works with and for this group); responsibility as administrator for program development and evaluation; sacramental catechesis for the whole community; and adult education and Rites of Christian Initiation for Adults.

What becomes immediately obvious is that this new person must be a member of a parish team, working with the special ministers of the community, the priests, sisters, deacons, school faculty, any of the many who serve others in the community. There are increasing numbers of persons trained by major centers of study in this field. Any diocesan office can provide a list of people available and the criteria required for the position of director of religious education.

DISASTER DRILLS
Disaster drills in catechetical programs? Yes! Disaster drills are necessary for the safety of any group which meets regularly in parish buildings, especially for the young and the aged who would be the most vulnerable in any accident.

Schools have a legal and moral obligation to have disaster drills. Many religion programs are run on a part-time basis, and there seems to be a strange—and dangerous—assumption that disaster won't strike during the "couple of hours a week we're in the building." A more accurate assumption is that since teachers and students are in the building only once or twice a week they may not be sure of the location of staircases, doors and exits. Disaster drills are essential.

Fire Drills
If the programs are in regular school buildings, the part-time staff and students should follow the established procedures of the school and the local fire department. Frequently fire-drill instructions are on the bulletin boards in each class. If the program is in a catechetical center, which may not come under school fire-safety regulations, invite local fire-safety personnel to the building to give advice on fire-drill procedures.

At the beginning of each year teachers and students need a tour of the building. Fire-drill rules should also be given at that time.

In an emergency the teacher makes sure that no one is left behind, closes the windows (if there is time) and closes the door. Safety demands that the teacher be the last one out of the room. This emphasizes the need for an aide in classes of younger children who need to be led out in an emergency.

The children must be taught how to leave the building and where to meet once the building is vacated. All teachers must have a roll book with them at all times. Everyone must be accounted for after the evacuation of the building. By using the roll book, personnel can quickly account for students actually missing in an emergency, not just absent that day.

Fire drills must be held early in the term. Teachers should be notified about the scheduled drill so that the lesson can be planned accordingly. At least one fire drill thereafter should be held unannounced to evaluate readiness.

Other Drills
Some areas are subject to certain natural disasters such as earthquakes or tornadoes. In those areas disaster drills should be part of the religious education program just as they are part of the school safety program. Instructions are usually posted in the classrooms and teacher-catechists should make a point of becoming familiar with the routine to be followed.

See also EMERGENCIES AND FIRST AID.

DISCIPLINE IN THE CLASSROOM

Most religious educators may feel a strangeness about the question of discipline in catechetics. How can we talk about the love of God and neighbor and yet be disciplinarians? Why do we have discipline problems in religion classes?

Problems arise for teacher-catechists when, during their first lesson on Jesus, Mary or prayer, the students get restless and distracted. Teachers who respond, "You must be good boys and girls in religion class," or with a raised voice and a show of temper are the problem.

Discipline, of course, is not just restrictions. It is control within the student, helped by rules agreed upon by the class and the teacher, and by the tone the teacher sets in this learning environment. More discipline problems are unconsciously precipitated by teachers than many of them realize.

It is helpful for teacher-catechists to hear their voices on audiotape (or, ideally, see and hear themselves on videotape) so that they know what impact they have on others. Teachers have an obligation to present themselves so that they don't interfere with students' learning.

A special note: New teacher-catechists need time and practice to achieve ease in group control. It is not automatic, but it can be learned, especially with help from more experienced teachers. Some students present particular problems. Don't hesitate to talk over difficult situations with the DRE or grade-level coordinator.

Here are some general observations and suggestions that can be considered in discipline strategies. They are not in order of priority; select what is most valuable for you.

‣ Keep your sense of humor.

‣ Plan lessons well. Be prepared.

‣ Motivate students by involving them in the planning of lessons, projects and activities.

‣ Know your students, their names and personalities.

‣ Explain rules. If you have no reason for a rule, don't make one. Have students participate in the rule-making process. Explain why rules are needed, and give students the opportunity to discuss rules they think are unfair or unnecessary.

‣ Provide variety in your presentation of material.

‣ Never leave a group unsupervised.

‣ Do not use threats that will never be carried out; for example, "You will sit here until you finish. I don't care if it takes all night."

‣ Never punish the group for the offense of an individual or a small group.

‣ Decide in advance the consequences of misbehavior and inform the students. Spur-of-the-moment penalties are unfair and often reflect the angry mood of the teacher rather than an appropriate response to the situation.

‣ Rules must apply to everyone.

‣ Establish procedures for routine classroom activities during the first days of class.

‣ Recognize your obligation to provide a safe and secure environment for the students. They should feel this concern.

‣ Give the students a preview of how time will be spent at the beginning of each session. Try to capture their interest.

‣ Give directions clearly. Otherwise, while you muffle through the directions, several self-appointed interpreters will begin translating your directions and a dozen questions will arise from every statement you make.

‣ Be consistent.

‣ Avoid name-calling, ridiculing, humiliating, discussing personal faults or problems in the presence of others, labelling students with titles such as "chatterbox," "class clown," "genius" or "troublemaker."

‣ Give the students the same respect and polite responses that you expect from them. Do not interrupt them while they are speaking or answering a question.

‣ Separate the person from the misbehavior or the action.

‣ Remember that "put-downs" are "put-offs."

‣ Remember that students model themselves on your behavior. Teachers who yell, who make wisecracks, who can't stand still, will see and hear themselves mirrored in the behavior of their students.

▸ Avoid bringing your ego into the classroom. Don't react to students' immature or insensitive remarks in such a way that the learning environment is distorted.

▸ Reflect after each class on what went well and what went wrong. Work out new approaches where needed.

▸ Remember how you acted when you were young and bored. Think about why you misbehaved or got in trouble. Look back and try to remember the classroom techniques used by a teacher that you enjoyed and utilize the best of these.

See also CLASSROOM MANAGEMENT, LESSON PLANS, MOTIVATION and NAMES.

DISCUSSION METHOD

As a classroom technique, the discussion approach has a lot to offer. Students in a formal question-and-answer dialogue with the teacher are prepared to give certain responses and to receive approval or disapproval; in the fairly unstructured freedom of a discussion, however, students are more spontaneous in their reactions to ideas, and reveal more accurately what they are thinking. Also, the more students talk about a topic within a group setting, the more frequently they will need to refine and redefine what they are thinking.

Discussions, of course, are common to any major interchange of ideas. The media talk frequently of "frank discussions" held in Rome, Geneva or Washington. In a labor mediation problem, we hear that "more discussions are planned for tomorrow."

The major concern for teacher-catechists is the phrase, "there were endless discussions," obviously not a positive sign. In some cases, unfortunately, students have grown accustomed to rambling, unconnected discussions that don't facilitate learning.

The *NCD* advocates the use of the discussion method at the adolescent and adult levels, but a good introduction should be made in the earlier grades. The teacher must decide if the students have enough background for discussion and, at the beginning, should instruct the students about ground rules and limits.

Discussion is a clarifying and stimulating technique. Through the exchange of opinions, the insertion of new ideas, and the challenge of differences, students sometimes can be brought to fever pitch. And, if discussion is well-handled, sides are not hardened but opened. Obviously the discussion leader is critical, and the general tone of the room is important.

A discussion is not meant to be a stage for setting off opinions or presenting dogmatic statements. It is the time to explore *together* through free and spontaneous talk and exchange. A few guidelines will help:

▸ The leader should keep the discussion under control; for example, it should not move into personalities, irrelevancies or non-sequiturs.

▸ Written or unwritten laws are needed; for example, who can talk and when.

▸ Keep the train of thought visible and viable. The leader can help by using a chalkboard or verbal comments for repetition, clarification and summary.

Although discussion is meant to be an exploration, it is not a bull session that starts and ends aimlessly. The topic is generally set and should cover material that the students can work with and make contributions to. (This does not preclude the spontaneous discussion that arises from time to time following a lecture or question-and-answer dialogue. That's wonderful. But discussions also can be planned.)

Perhaps the most difficult aspect of the discussion method is controlling disagreement or sharp answers that may seem unfriendly or even vindictive. However, practice with discussions, and the general tone set by the group, will help eliminate or ease that problem.

See also QUESTION-AND-ANSWER METHOD.

DRAMA

People of every age and place have presented stories and ideas in a dramatic way to teach, to entertain and to help communities understand themselves. Dramatic representations are among our most creative ways of understanding who we are.

The use of drama is indispensable to good teaching. Through this medium the teacher-catechist can utilize the creative aspects of children and adolescents and help them discover, re-create or rethink the meanings and messages of their lives and traditions.

Many forms of dramatic expression are available for use in the classroom or parish setting: plays, pantomimes, improvisations, role plays, complete-a-skits, tableaux. All these involve students in expression, communication, celebration, clarification and formulation of values. They represent treasured stories, parables and traditions, bringing them to new levels of learning and appreciation.

The value of drama for catechetics, however, is in its creativity, spontaneity, fantasy and festivity. Before initiating a dramatic play activity, teachers need to free themselves of the images of the latest Broadway production. Teacher-catechists need to concentrate on the *play* aspect of the experience. Production is not the key; playfulness which brings forth learning is the approach.

Plays range from formal presentations, memorized or read from a script, to the idea of playing a story. The latter is somewhat reminiscent of children at play; for example, playing house, store or school.

Pantomime uses actions and gestures without words to convey meaning, express thoughts and communicate feelings. The age-old parlor game of charades, Marcel Marceau, and Shields and Yarnell come to mind when we think of pantomime.

Improvisation is an extemporaneous form of dramatic expression. A given story is enacted with little preparation. Improvisation encourages spontaneity.

Role plays give students a chance to pretend to be other people and to fantasize what they would do in a particular situation. Participants are asked to characterize someone. The person's behavior is usually a response to a staged predicament which calls for a solution or resolution.

Complete-a-skits are role plays in which the developing action is set in a script but the ending is left open. The story line is usually written to precipitate ideas for a variety of creative endings. Complete-a-skits are frequently used in value education.

Tableaux depict in still life a story or a scene from a story. Characters hold set positions while a narrator or a song relates the story.

Finger plays are written for or composed by young children. Words are given for each finger to tell a story. Fingers are sometimes given names like "Thumbkin," "Pointer" and "Pinky." This form is exciting for very young students.

Some suggested resources:
Child's Play and *Doing, Dance and Drama* (Ave Maria Press); *Jesus Plays for Primary Grades* (Twenty-Third Publications).

See also EXPERIENTIAL APPROACH and PLAY.

DUPLICATING MATERIALS AND METHODS

We are in the age of the handout, that convenient sheet of paper. With handouts each student has a worksheet, a copy of the story, a script or the same illustration.

Two items are of importance to teacher-catechists: the various *machines* that provide instant or fairly instant material for every student; and the *content* of these various sheets, especially those found in duplicating books, spirit-master books and the special pullout sheets made for copying.

First, a brief word on the machines. If the program has its own duplicating or reproducing equipment, guides for use and operation are critical. Programs often depend upon working machines with sufficient supplies. Give careful directions (and follow them). Also, as a rule, research the pros and cons of each type of equipment prior to budgeting funds or making any major purchase. The choice of equipment should not be left to the DRE alone unless that person has had special training or experience; help from the advisory board or some knowledgeable and experienced people in the community is critical.

Second, some comments on types and quality of duplicating material. Some companies publish books of lessons, pictures, puzzles, games, tests, charts and almost anything else you can think of in the spirit-master format. The teaching catechist simply tears out the page selected and duplicates copies for each student on any liquid or spirit-type direct-process duplicator. Clear or blank spirit-master units also can be purchased by the box, and can be used to produce anything that can be typed, printed, written, drawn or traced upon the spirit master with a ball point pen.

A number of publishers now market materials that can be reproduced by some form of photocopy and grant subscribers or purchasers of the material the right to reproduce it for classroom use.

Before investing money in spirit-master books, carefully review and evaluate them. Be sure that the activities on these convenient sheets relate to religious education and are not simply language-arts activities or games without any application to religious education.

When selecting from the many spirit-master books, evaluate each page to find out how it relates to the theme of the lesson. Teacher-catechists can also prepare homemade master sheets that introduce, help clarify or reinforce lessons in a more creative and beneficial way than some of the prepared materials.

There are many real "finds" for a busy classroom teacher among the prepared materials, but there is such an unevenness about these materials that we feel it important to advise teacher-catechists to review each sheet before using it and to look over the entire collection in any book to make sure it's worth the purchase price.

See also BUSY-WORK AND GIMMICKS.

E

He had gone into the Temple and was teaching, when the chief priests and the elders of the people came to him and said, "What authority have you for acting like this?" (Mt 21:23).

E

EARLY CHILDHOOD PROGRAMS

A 20th-century achievement is the discovery of inner space, the exploration of the workings and development of the human mind. In the past children were thought of as "little adults" whose thinking and acting were small-scale adult functions. It is now known that children become adults through gradual stages of physical, social, emotional, moral and mental growth.

Thinking about the early preschool years of learning has changed as a result of this understanding of development. Before, many people thought that these years were not significant, that no real learning occurred. The work of Jean Piaget brought the critical years of early childhood into a new focus. Piaget's observations of the developing child offer insights into how children go about the business of "learning to know, learning the methods of concept formation." Piaget states that children learn concepts only as they develop through stages which are "sequential in nature and biologically based."

What effect does this have on catechetics? It has moved some to look at the preschool experiences of children in the parish and explore religious education possibilities in early childhood. It has also resulted in studies of faith development and moral development (see DEVELOPMENTAL PSYCHOLOGY—James Fowler, Lawrence Kohlberg).

The *NCD* stresses the role of the family in early childhood development and also suggests that catechetical programs for 3- to 5-year-olds "seek to foster their growth in a wider faith community." Preschool programs must allow children "to develop at their own pace, in ways suited to their age, circumstances, and learning abilities" (No. 177).

Teacher-catechists working with early childhood programs must have some knowledge and understanding of the development of preschool children. This understanding will help them in preparing lessons and activities that deepen children's sense of awe and wonder, that engage them in activities appropriate for their level of motor skill development, and that allow play its role in learning.

Some informative readings include *Christian Child Development* (Harper and Row) and *The Religious Education of Preschool Children* (Religious Education Press).

See also EXPERIENTIAL APPROACH and PLAY.

EASTER

There's an adult solemnity about Easter that children have difficulty with, and teachers must remember that some students do not understand why Easter is a greater feast than Christmas.

Teachers should not be impatient. For most people a baby's birth is a close and immediate experience of joy. The feast of Christmas is easy to relate to children. The experience of death and resurrection, however, requires mature faith. To understand Easter, understanding the events of Good Friday is necessary. Young students have difficulty with understanding death and suffering. Teacher-catechists can only prepare them for this faith experience by sharing their own sense of the life and joy and excitement of Easter. We are an "Easter people," an "alleluia community," and youngsters must know more about this special mystery.

From the point of view of catechetical programs, advance preparations for the Easter ceremonies are essential. In this age of the electric light, the paschal candle is not as dramatic a phenomenon as in the past; water and oil are not obvious signs of life and healing to today's students. They need to hear the stories of people in passage to understand the signs used in the liturgy, and they need to experience some of the activities that show new life and hope.

During Lent and Holy Week, lessons should focus on the experience of death to life through appropriate prayers and activities. The cycles in nature, the symbols of baptism, and Old Testament accounts of the Exodus are good lesson themes. Celebrating a seder meal, dramatizing the stations of the cross, making baptismal robes and decorating eggs with signs of Christian renewal are excellent classroom activities that help prepare students for the liturgy of Easter and the experience of joy.

Students need help with the Easter music. Allow time to familiarize them with the traditional hymns and alleluias so they can join with the community's celebration.

Since Easter is the beginning of the paschal season, Easter lessons and activities should continue throughout the season. Classes should have the opportunity to see the paschal candle, visit the baptismal font and find Easter symbols in church. If we put Easter away quickly, our students will think accordingly. Pentecost is the logical climax of this season; special care must be taken that catechetical programs don't ignore this feast because it does not fit into the school calendar.

See also LENT, HOLY WEEK and PENTECOST.

ECUMENISM

For a long time, many American Catholics learned that their church was separate and right. But there was more separateness and righteousness than should be characteristic of a Christlike community.

The separate church of those years and the historical reasons for our illusion of possessing the complete truth have been the subject of many learned articles. In the second half of this century, under the impetus of Pope John XXIII, we began a dialogue with the rest of the world churches. The *NCD* discusses this movement in a section entitled "The Church in Dialogue" (No. 755ff.). It is a section that teacher-catechists should use for reflection and as a call to action as well.

"The Church in Dialogue" stresses that catechesis is to be "sensitive" to others. It encourages catechists to present "information about other Christians honestly and accurately, avoiding words, judgments, and actions which misrepresent their beliefs and practices."

It also encourages "ecumenical dialogue and common prayer, especially public and private prayers for unity." Teachers should make a point of studying additional passages which discuss the Jewish community, the Moslem peoples, other religions and those who profess no religion.

Genuine love of others and acceptance of differences among people are essential to an ecumenical thrust in catechetics. Attitudes are communicated in the classroom, and teachers should be very conscious of this when discussing other religions.

Signs of ecumenism are seen in the increasingly public dialogue among religious leaders and the sharing of public worship among churches. There is more ecumenical dialogue in adult education programs, more study of other religions in the senior and junior high school classes, and a general acceptance of other religious groups in our attitudes.

Religions of the World (ROA) is a 10-episode filmstrip set that can be used for junior and senior high school students, and adults, as an introduction to ecumenical studies.

EDUCATIONAL PSYCHOLOGY

Educational psychology covers all areas in the field of psychology that bear upon learning, both in its normal stages and in special education. It includes human development, theories of learning, motivation, memory, transfer of learning, discipline, evaluation, social and individual differences. More and more emphasis is being given in church documents to the contributions that psychology gives to the teaching/learning processes.

The complexity of the learning process and the many aspects of student and teacher behavior that teaching catechists must consider are evident. A tendency in the past placed the burden of learning on the students and made them adjust to the teacher. The contribution of the behavioral sciences, especially psychology, has been to help teachers see, with more precision, the importance of human development in the learning process.

Most texts today apply the general findings

of educational psychology in choosing appropriate material. Teachers, however, need to be prepared to follow the suggestions of the authors through understanding and assimilating the basics of educational psychology. All dioceses should give sufficient place to educational psychology in their teacher-training programs.

See also LEARNING THEORY, DEVELOPMENTAL PSYCHOLOGY, MOTIVATION, EXPERIENTIAL APPROACH and DISCIPLINE IN THE CLASSROOM.

ELECTIVE COURSES

Junior and senior high school students enjoy choosing their courses and generally profit from having some responsibility for their programs. Elective offerings, a practice endorsed by the NCD (No. 232) for Catholic schools, can be adapted to all parish religious education programs for adults and adolescents.

One elective plan, for example, divides the school year into "mini-semesters" of six to eight weeks. Teachers and themes change each period. Students register for the courses they want each semester. This approach meets the need for change and choice and helps students avoid repetition and boredom.

Electives require more complex scheduling and staffing, but the success in terms of student motivation and interest must be considered. Teachers also have the advantage of choosing to teach topics that they enjoy in their area of expertise.

Some parishes that offer elective courses prepare schedules with course descriptions and instructors listed. These are sent to the students before registration, giving them time to think about and plan their own programs.

Some continuity must be built into elective programming. Records that include information about what electives were taken, when they were taken and with whom must be kept for each student in the program. The course descriptions for each year should be kept on file in the religious education office. Long-range planning and good record keeping help insure substantial, non-repetitive elective offerings for at least a four-year cycle.

See CONTRACT LEARNING, HIGH SCHOOL PROGRAMS and YOUTH MINISTRY.

ELEMENTARY PROGRAMS

For most people schooling began at the age of six when they entered first grade for the basic elements of learning. Educators agree that most 6-year-olds have a "readiness" for reading and writing that comes with the physical and intellectual development of that age. The cognitive structure, however, of elementary-age children makes it difficult for them to understand abstract concepts. They tend to translate abstractions into concrete terms and to miss connections.

In elementary religious education we are often guilty of giving too much, too soon. Elementary-age students are given the full content of the faith in case they do not continue their religious education after confirmation or completion of the elementary program. In the eagerness to share the message of Jesus, the developmental abilities of the students are not always taken into consideration. (This compares somewhat to pushing courses on the works of Shakespeare on fourth-graders because they might drop out before high school.)

The NCD, in its guidelines for childhood development (ages 6 to 10), reminds teachers that "intellectual capacity *gradually* expands," and that this is a period of growth and not finality. "Certain prayer formulas become *more* intelligible. . . . Parables take on *deeper* meanings. . . . Sharing and helping others make a great deal *more* sense" (No. 178, italics added).

Catechists teaching in elementary programs find this a stage of development when students learn largely through experiences with and by others. "In presenting the values and teachings of Jesus, catechesis takes note of children's experience and encourages them to apply the same teachings and values to their lives" (No. 178).

Publishers of religious education materials generally have the bulk of the texts geared to the elementary grades. Materials are adapted to the developmental and interest levels of first-through sixth-graders. Characteristics of each developmental stage are included in the teacher's manuals.

Elementary programs in religious education should be just that—a good beginning. They should create positive attitudes toward religious education, stirring a genuine interest in growing in wisdom and knowledge.

An excellent book for early childhood and elementary teachers is *Readiness for Religion* (Seabury).

See also DEVELOPMENTAL PSYCHOLOGY and EXPERIENTIAL APPROACH.

EMERGENCIES AND FIRST AID

Teachers in full or part-time programs realize safeguards for the physical well-being of the students require carefully planned procedures. Arrangements must be made by the DRE with the help of the teachers, aides and parents.

1) Obtain special information needed by the staff from the parents at registration. All student forms should have telephone numbers where the parents can be contacted in case of emergency. Home and work numbers should be given, and also the number of a relative or friend who will accept responsibility for the child if the parents cannot be reached in an emergency. A doctor's number should also be included.

2) Post, in the main office, telephone numbers for emergency aid, police, fire department, ambulance service and poison control.

3) The DRE should interview the staff and note all personnel who have training in medical services, first aid and coronary-pulmonary resuscitation (CPR). Post the skill and the room where each person can be found during program hours.

4) Each religious education office should have a first-aid kit for cuts, scratches, burns and bites. Remind teachers and staff that they

are not permitted to administer any type of medication to students.

5) Advise the staff, in writing and at meetings, of emergency procedures. On the first day each teacher should select a student or aide who will go to the main office for assistance if a student is hurt or sick in the classroom. Teachers must remember to stay with the sick child, to remain with the class, and to send for help, not go for it.

6) The parish should include all religious education programs in insurance coverage. Make insurance information known to staff, parents and all adult participants.

See also DISASTER DRILLS.

EUCHARIST

The Eucharist is a lifelong and ongoing sacrament, a sign of unity and community, a bond for today and a remembrance of yesterday, a meal of thanksgiving and a pledge of future life. This sacrament, the most frequent and common public experience in the church, demands the most catechetical attention from its first reception through each stage of our lives.

The major concentrated eucharistic effort in parishes generally has been on first communion programs. For some, the most noticeable catechetical changes have been with communion and penance preparation and reception.

Family and community practices and customs for first communion are still very strong. In some places there are long-established traditions that do not reflect the theology and liturgical reforms of Vatican II. Teaching catechists are conscious from their own experiences that many parents and grandparents see their child's first communion as a sign of continuity with their own lives. First communion is not only the introduction of a child into fuller community participation; it is also a reminder to adults of their own faith commitment.

The *NCD* offers directions in sacramental preparation that involve parents more actively. Priests, DREs and teaching catechists help parishioners reflect and evaluate customs and practices in light of the changes in sacramental thinking.

Perhaps the most significant change has been the acknowledgment of how children think at the age of 7. Formerly we gave second-graders fully worked out belief formulas to be memorized. These formulas were very difficult for them to understand and assimilate. The *NCD* states that "children around the age of 7 tend to think concretely; they grasp concepts like 'unity' and 'belonging' from experiences, such as sharing, listening, eating, conversing, giving, thanking, and celebrating." This means that children begin the process of understanding by talking about their own experiences; it calls for sacramental explanations "adapted to their intellectual capacity." From these beginnings, the children will receive Christ's body and blood in an "informed and reverent manner" (No. 122).

Because children think concretely, they have difficulty with the abstract concept of the physical presence of Jesus within them. They only begin to understand Eucharist from their experiences of love and friendship.

The texts used for most communion preparations reflect this thinking and provide material appropriate to the developmental levels of the students. The books familiarize the children with the events of Jesus' life and the actions of the Mass. Teaching activities should include experiences of celebration and involvement. Scheduled trips to the church to let the children see and touch the things they normally only experience from a distance help them understand more about the liturgical actions of the community. Meetings with a priest to talk about what he does give children an opportunity to ask questions about what they see, hear and think.

The DRE and the teachers working with communion classes can also assist adults in examining family and community communion customs. Some practices make it difficult for youngsters to focus on the meaning of communion. Sometimes parent and teacher expectations are communicated to the children and cause unnecessary excitement and anxiety. There may be an exaggerated emphasis on communion outfits, photography sessions, parties and gifts. Long rehearsals may put too much emphasis on externals. The question of rehearsals, special dresses and suits and even photographers must be evaluated in terms of the community's idea of what the sacrament means and how it is celebrated. Parent meetings should not be taken up with shopping for first communion "accessories."

The scheduling of more first communion liturgies allows for smaller groups and a variety of approaches. Smaller groups afford students a more personal liturgical experience and provide families more opportunities for active participation. First communicants can be prepared to join in the readings, prayers, processions and music.

The move toward more parental involvement in communion preparation and liturgy brings with it some special concerns. One-parent families and non-Catholic parents should not be put in uncomfortable situations.

Since Eucharist is the "heart of Christian life," religious education programs must continue to foster growth, understanding and positive experiences of this sacrament. The *NCD* points out that from understanding brought through catechesis, members of the community will express their life in Christ with "works of charity, service, missionary activity, and witness" (No. 121).

The process of discovering contemporary worship continues at the adult level. With the changes in language and structure allowed by Vatican II certain customs no longer suitable were dropped. Because the familiar is hard to lose, many lost heart at the new forms. These forms are taking time to develop. Parish catechesis should help people continue to grow in understanding of Eucharist through homilies, study groups, adult education, prayer and discussion sessions.

EVANGELIZATION

To many Christians the word *evangelization* is related to the four gospel writers, the evangelists. For some, it applies more appropriately to mission magazine stories or storefront churches.

In *Evangelization in the Modern World* (1975) Paul VI advised *all* the faithful to lay the groundwork for the gospel message through evangelization. This laying of the groundwork can be compared to the educational concept of readiness for learning. We are becoming more aware of the need people have to be prepared for certain experiences. Evangelization is a readiness process which is necessary before personal acceptance of the gospel.

There are points in life when people are more disposed, by reason of maturing or circumstances, to be open to ideas and suggestions. To know when a person is ready to listen indicates an understanding of motivation, of the drives that help a person be ready and willing to change behavior and thinking. Evangelization is more than the proclamation of the good news of Jesus. It seeks to understand the hearers' needs and to provide materials people need and want to change and grow.

The *NCD* makes a distinction between evangelization and catechesis. Evangelization has as its purpose the "arousing of the beginnings of faith"; catechesis refers to "those efforts that help individuals and communities acquire and deepen faith." Catechesis presupposes evangelization (readiness). Teaching catechists are frequently aware of baptized students in their classes who have not committed their lives to Christ. There must be an effort in catechetical programs to bring about personal witnessing to Christ.

As the *NCD* tells us, we are now in an era where evangelization is not a call to the foreign pagan but, rather, to the community present to us. More people are coming together to explore the meaning of evangelization in American life. A growing number of large-scale meetings, and the publications and movements within parishes, indicate a renewed dimension in church life today.

In this work our attention is directed to the ongoing process of catechesis for which pre-evangelization and evangelization are essential prerequisites. "Like evangelization, catechesis is incomplete if it does not take into account the constant interplay between gospel teaching and human experience—individual and social, personal and institutional, sacred and secular" (*NCD*, No. 35).

EXAMINATIONS AND EVALUATIONS

Many teacher-catechists are quite ambivalent about testing and grading students, using report cards, or awarding prizes for achievement. Some say that a teacher's role in religious education is not to evaluate a student's faith or examine his or her beliefs. On the other hand, a body of knowledge exists and is taught in class. A factor in teaching religion is to determine what students actually know in order to decide what must be taught. Teachers cannot build on an unknown foundation, and testing is one way to find out where each student is.

Especially for teachers of large groups examinations are a manageable way of checking what knowledge has been acquired and remembered. Not many programs have the luxury of a one-to-one student-teacher ratio where each student can be personally interviewed about what has been taught.

How examinations are used by teachers and what students learn from them determine their value and effectiveness in religious education. In our own work with students we test to see if they have begun to assimilate and adapt facts, concepts, principles and attitudes. We use essay questions, appropriate to the age and background of the group, and ask reflective questions. We talk to the students about their responses and write comments on their papers emphasizing what is positive. We tell the students that examinations are designed to help them see what they know and don't know and to give them an opportunity to express their ideas on subjects discussed in class.

Examinations provide some challenge and motivation to absorb content that is needed for adult life. Most children enjoy an opportunity to show what they have learned. In the early years of learning children are always committing data to memory, and the memorization of religious educational material (related to meaning) is an asset for adult life. (See MEMORIZATION.)

Evaluations are also an important aspect of religious education. Some programs use report cards as the normal form of evaluation. The first consideration is what type of information about the students is needed and by whom. Parents have a right and a need to know what their children are doing. Some communication about learning, participation, readiness, attendance, attitudes, and so forth, can be given to the parents.

Informal chats with parents cannot always replace some type of formal communication. Since not every parent is free to visit classes, there is an obligation on the part of teaching catechists to share their evaluations of the students' understanding of the course content and attitudes in religious education with parents. Each program must decide on the form of the evaluations given to parents or guardians, and what type of parish records should be kept.

A related question involves evaluation of students by teachers for the next grade level. It is important that a student have a right to a fresh start with each new term; it is also important that a teacher know what to prepare for the class coming up. Teachers should communicate important information—attendance, report cards, material covered and behavioral problems—to the next teacher. A good teacher gets to know a class as individuals growing each year, but an experienced teacher also appreciates knowing what to prepare for.

Do examinations belong in every class and in each program? Common sense will dictate that small group discussion, for example, may not need formal examinations and evaluations. This approach too, however, should be accountable in some way for its time and impact on students, and there should be some communication with parents about what has gone on.

The wide range of possibilities in catechetics, from the free-flowing small group to the more traditional classroom, from the formal preparation for Eucharist and confirmation to middle school projects, all call for evaluation of the students' levels and communication and record-keeping about the students' work.

EXPERIENTIAL APPROACH

The expression, Experience is the best teacher, is true, but it must be remembered that some people never learn from their own experiences because they have never thought about them or were never helped with them. Perhaps we should say, The best teacher is the one who helps us with our experiences. That is how we really learn.

The experiential approach to learning is very important. For too long, both in secular and religious education, learning was separate from doing and was not connected to children's experiences. Real learning was thought to take place when students sat still, listened and were passively absorbed in an "intellectual manner." Play and activities were thought to be unnecessary and unrelated to intellectual growth.

We are now discovering from such pioneers as John Dewey of Columbia University and Thomas Edward Shields of Catholic University that learning is related to children's experiences and is built on their active use of all their faculties—reason, imagination, emotions and senses. Children learn by doing. The role of the teacher is twofold: to use the children's experiences and to provide opportunities for new experiences.

Teachers have learned that the highest percentage of learning takes place when students are actively involved in the process. It occurs when the children talk about what they already know and begin to utilize their own skills and experiences in moving forward with new situations.

The *NCD* endorses this wholeheartedly:

> Experience is of great importance in catechesis. Experiential learning . . . gives rise to concerns and questions, hopes and anxieties, reflections and judgments, which increase one's desire to penetrate more deeply into life's meaning. . . . The experiential approach is not easy, but it can be of considerable value to catechesis. Catechists should encourage people to reflect on their significant experiences. . . . Sometimes they will provide appropriate experiences. . . (*NCD*, No. 176d).

"Appropriate experiences" include activities, projects and celebrations that provide students with opportunities to bring themselves into the learning situation. This educational methodology depends upon understanding what the students' developmental levels are and what actions and involvement are appropriate. From classroom and parish activities, teacher-catechists should help students *"observe, explore, interpret* and *judge* their experiences, *ascribe* a Christian meaning to their lives and *act* according to the norms of faith and love" (*NCD*, No. 181, italics added).

These are action words and it is with the experiential approach to learning that they will have life in the classroom and in the students.

See also EDUCATIONAL PSYCHOLOGY, DEVELOPMENTAL PSYCHOLOGY, FIELD TRIPS and PLAY.

F

FACILITIES

FACULTY MEETINGS

FIELD TRIPS

Fire Drills
   (see DISASTER DRILLS)

First Aid
   (see EMERGENCIES AND FIRST AID)

G

Good News
   (see BIBLE)

GRADE-LEVEL COORDINATORS

GRADE-LEVEL SYSTEM

Grading
   (see EXAMINATIONS AND EVALUATIONS)

Guest Speakers
   (see RESOURCE PEOPLE)

Using many parables like these, he spoke the word to them, so far as they were capable of understanding it. He would not speak to them except in parables, but he explained everything to his disciples when they were alone (Mk 4:33-34).

F

FACILITIES

In an end-of-the-year evaluation a DRE asked teacher-catechists: "What was the greatest difficulty you encountered as a teacher?" Much to the DRE's surprise, a large number of teachers responded: "Using someone else's classroom."

The National Inventory of Parish Catechetical Programs indicates that most religious education programs are placed in shared facilities. This poses a lot of nitty-gritty problems.

Some common complaints from teachers using classrooms of a Catholic school include not being able to move desks, write on boards, store anything in the room from one week to the next, display students' work, open windows, use the coat closet, change the position of the shades or use the pencil sharpener.

The full-time teachers whose rooms were used complained about projects being moved; things missing from desks, lockers and coat closets; desks left out of order; windows left open; and equipment broken and not reported.

Sharing obviously causes problems. Guidelines and channels of communication must be worked out. This usually involves a number of people—the full-time teacher, the teaching catechist, the DRE, the principal of the Catholic school and possibly the maintenance person. Guidelines should be formulated *before* classes begin.

Difficulties specific to the sharing situation in the particular parish should be identified. Any remedy must reflect the principles of Christian community and purpose. Disputes over shared facilities are, unfortunately, often a sign of a broader conflict existing between a CCD program and the Catholic school.

See also LIBRARY AND RELIGIOUS EDUCATION RESOURCE ROOM.

FACULTY MEETINGS

Faculty meetings are important for communication, and their effectiveness for teachers depends upon the quality and type of meetings held. Whether the meetings are formal or informal (and both types should be part of every program), teachers must feel they have gained something from participating—new ideas, renewed spirit, support, opportunities to share problems and successes.

To insure maximum participation, DREs must provide an advance notice of the meeting, an agenda and approximate time the meeting is expected to last. Interminable sessions are the sure death of faculty meetings and can precipitate the loss of teachers. "I would love to teach in our CCD program, but I just don't have the time to sit at those endless, waste-of-time meetings," is a complaint of potential and drop-out teachers.

Scheduling faculty meetings depends upon the DRE's understanding of the staff's schedules and needs. Some teachers can come an hour before class for meetings; others prefer to stay after the teaching session. Some DREs report success in arranging meetings on non-teaching days or evenings. Others program the same meeting twice, once during the day and again in the evening. (This is also done for parent meetings.)

Instead of general meetings each month some DREs schedule grade-level meetings with the teachers of the same grade or division—primary, intermediate, etc. General meetings are scheduled for the beginning of the sessions, for Advent and Christmas lesson ideas and schedules, for Lent and Easter programs, and for an end-of-the-year business/social get-together.

Distributing teacher's notes or minutes of the meetings to those who were unable to attend a particular session is an invaluable way to include everyone.

Teachers also need opportunities to get together for shared prayer and socializing. They should have a place to meet informally and spontaneously before and after classes where a coffeepot welcomes them.

See also IN-SERVICE TRAINING.

FIELD TRIPS

The experiential approach makes a strong effort to involve students in the learning process. Field trips, well planned and executed, bring students to a learning situation where they can see and do many things that involve religious education themes.

The *NCD* suggests "such things as field trips, meaningful social action, weekend retreats and programs" as means to provide "continued opportunities for concrete experiences of lived faith, in which the message of salvation is applied to specific situations" (No. 181).

Teacher-catechists of each grade level should meet at the beginning of the school year to plan field trips for their group. Students' ages, curriculum themes and local resources must be considered in the planning session. Older students should be included in the planning for their field trips.

Every locale has special places and groups to visit. For example, New York students can visit the Catholic Worker Movement, the United Nations, St. John the Divine and St. Patrick's, or meet with the Brothers of Taize. Washington area students can visit the Trappists in Berryville, the National Shrine of the Immaculate Conception or the Emmaus House. Each diocese has agencies that offer not only places to visit but opportunities for social action; for example, Catholic Charities, homes for the homeless, the aged and infirm, and other service institutions. Motherhouses and seminaries also can be found in most dioceses.

The parish compound provides places for the younger children to visit. Children enjoy guided tours of the church, sacristy, choir, sanctuary and side altars. The convent, rectory, the religious education office and a parish collection center for the poor can all be visited during primary-grade field trips. Classes can arrange to be present for a baptism, marriage or anointing of the sick in the parish.

Neighboring churches and synagogues, gardens and parks, museums, plays, movies and concerts may serve for field trips related to various catechetical themes.

Before a class goes on a field trip, the students must be prepared for the experience.

The teaching catechist can ready a group by discussing where they will be going; what they might see, do and experience; the day's agenda, including time, meeting places and possible costs; and appropriate behavior for the situation. The teacher should send home permission slips to be signed by parents or guardians at least a few days before the trip. All students leaving the parish compound during religious education sessions need written permission.

See also EXPERIENTIAL APPROACH.

G

GRADE-LEVEL COORDINATORS

Some religious education programs have initiated the position of grade-level coordinator and found it quite successful. This person is generally an experienced teacher of a particular grade who works closely with the DRE and the faculty of the same grade level. In parishes where only one or two sections of a grade exist, the same concept is applied to clusters of grades, for example, preschool, primary, intermediate, junior and senior high.

Grade-level coordinators arrange meetings for sharing ideas with all the teachers of their group. They also serve a critical function, especially in larger parishes, as liaison to the rest of the program, the advisory board, and the DRE when problems or decisions common to the program arise.

Many of the concerns of new teachers are handled by the coordinator. In fact, many parishes report great success in recruiting new teachers through a coordinator. The new teacher has a sense of *we will be doing this together* and is assured of personal help and attention.

The coordinator oversees cooperative course planning, material selection, liturgy preparations, and special group projects and activities for his or her grade level. Small communities are frequently established among teachers who work together with a coordinator as they share common goals and interests.

Parishes with religious education advisory boards use grade-level coordinators as members of the board. Their contact with students and teachers and their awareness of grade-level problems make them good representatives. The religious education representative on the parish council is sometimes elected from among grade-level coordinators.

See also ADVISORY BOARD.

GRADE-LEVEL SYSTEM

Most religious education programs for children and youth are organized according to the grade-level system used in schools. Starting with kindergarten for the 5-year-olds, grades proceed from first to 12th with the students spending a year in each grade.

Individual differences are manifested in every class. Teachers must make adjustments to suit the needs of the more gifted, the less enthusiastic, the physically immature and those with learning disabilities.

For religious educators there are some disadvantages to consider in grade-level groupings. Promotion and retention, lock-step movement from one grade to the next, completion of material within a designated curriculum and time span, and other common grade-level pro-cedures are not necessarily effective in religious education.

Assigning students by grade levels poses another problem as well. Where do you place a third-grader who has never attended religion class? Some administrators place the student in the first grade; others let the child stay with the third-graders. The first solution is complicated by the interest level, reading ability and the pride of a third-grader sitting in a first-grade class. The second solution offers little help to a child who missed a sacramental preparation class in the second or third grade.

Many publishing companies, in an effort to help teaching catechists ease this problem, provide materials for students with little or no formal religious education. These non-graded programs provide summary-type materials for those about to enter graded programs and in need of preliminary instruction. They also offer sacramental preparation programs for a variety of developmental levels.

Some parishes offer classes prepared according to themes for students within a given age range instead of a system of grade level. Others group students according to interests and abilities, stressing small-group sessions and individualization. Contract learning provides a form of individualization (see CONTRACT LEARNING). Many parishes have developed a core of volunteer catechists who are willing to work on a one-to-one basis with students. Other communities work totally in family catechetics.

H

HANDBOOKS
HANDICAPPED
HIGH SCHOOL PROGRAMS
HOLY DAYS AND HOLIDAYS
HOLY ORDERS
HOLY WEEK
HOME CLASSES
HOMEWORK
HOMILIES
Human Development
   (see DEVELOPMENTAL PSYCHOLOGY)
Humanism (see LEARNING THEORY)

I

IN-SERVICE TRAINING

He taught in the Temple every day. The chief priests and the scribes, with the support of the leading citizens, tried to do away with him, but they did not see how they could carry this out because the people as a whole hung on his words (Lk 19:47-48).

H

HANDBOOKS

Many religious education programs give each family a handbook at registration time. Teacher-catechists should also have their own copy. Handbooks provide information and help people become comfortable with and knowledgeable about the religious education program.

Most handbooks include:

▸ basic goals of the program

▸ a list of courses and activities offered

▸ a description of the curriculum for each grade level (scope and sequence)

▸ parish policy for sacramental preparation and reception

▸ class schedules—starting and dismissal times, days off, policy for inclement weather

▸ emergency and safety procedures

▸ policy about attendance, conduct, homework, evaluations and report cards (if any)

▸ list of staff, telephone numbers and office locations

▸ religious education office and library hours

▸ any other information the staff, including the teachers, thinks is necessary

A well-prepared handbook does not have to be revised each year. Inserts, such as a calendar, can be prepared annually.

See also COMMUNICATIONS.

HANDICAPPED

The *NCD* reminds us that approximately 12½ percent of the population is in some way handicapped and that this group has needs which teacher-catechists must be prepared to meet. Every parish community has the blind, the deaf, the paralyzed, the mentally retarded, the emotionally disturbed, and those with learning disabilities. Some are permanently handicapped; others have temporary disabilities.

Each community, however, differs little from the communities Jesus taught, with the deaf, the blind and the lame all having the gospel preached to them. To teach as Jesus did, catechists must be ready to work with the handicapped too.

Secular educators have long debated the question of *mainstreaming*, that is, placing physically or emotionally handicapped people into regular programs rather than segregating them because of their special needs and problems. The church cautions religious educators not to segregate the handicapped excessively or unnecessarily. Common sense must be combined with efforts to make adjustments in facilities and programs in order to make mainstreaming a reality for the handicapped.

Special training and materials are sometimes needed by catechists who teach the handicapped. The following resources should be considered.

For the Blind

The Xavier Society for the Blind provides a direct, free service for the visually impaired. It provides large-print, braille and tape-text versions of books which are used in religious education programs. The texts are loaned for a semester or an entire school year. The materials are geared to the level required by the individual student.

The society strongly encourages religious education directors and teachers to invite the visually impaired into their programs. The Xavier Society will make available any books needed in the course. For information about the religion textbook program, the free lending library or other services offered, write to the Xavier Society for the Blind, 154 East 32nd Street, New York, New York 10010.

For the Deaf

The International Catholic Deaf Association has offered grants for assistance to the deaf, including funds for the training of catechists who teach the deaf. Among those groups receiving this type of assistance is the Catholic Deaf Apostolate, 243 Steele Road, West Hartford, Connecticut 06117.

Religious education and ministry-to-the-deaf workshops have become more available to catechists in various dioceses. Check with your local diocesan office.

Gallaudet College, Kendall Green, Washington, D.C. 20002, has a list of religious education periodicals that can be found in their college library. It is a multidenominational listing for the deaf that includes almost all the available periodicals. One periodical, *Listening,* is directed toward the "Catholic Black Deaf Community, a Minority within a Minority." It is published by the National Catholic Office for the Deaf, Trinity College, Washington, D.C. 20027.

With some assistance, parishes can set up a variety of programs for deaf adults, youth and children. Many parish volunteers have hidden talents; directors of religious education, when interviewing catechists for teaching positions, often find people who know deaf communications like Siglish, Ameslan, the manual alphabet or lip reading. Many community colleges and adult evening programs offer courses in deaf communication that would be helpful to catechists interested in but not trained for working with the deaf.

Special Religious Education
Those working in special religious education will find many sources of information and assistance. Here are but a few.

SPRED (Special Religious Education) is a newsletter published monthly (Sept. through May) by the Office of Religious Education of the Archdiocese of Chicago, 1025 West Fry Street, Chicago, Illinois 60622. Its articles cover a wide range of special education situations: the handicapped, developmental disabilities, mental health problems, learning disabilities, blindness, deafness and other physical disabilities.

SPRED also publishes handbooks used in its program for training catechists. *Faith and the Mentally Retarded: The Chicago Experience* gives the history of the program's beginnings, the research and the experimentation. It can be ordered from Current Catechetical Development, 6049 West Nelson Street, Chicago, Illinois 60634.

The National Apostolate for the Mentally

Retarded, 211 Steele St., West Hartford, Connecticut 06117, also publishes a newsletter and bibliography of resources specifically for the problems of the mentally retarded.

A booklet, *Recognizing and Helping the Learning Disabled Child in Your Classroom* is published by the National Catholic Education Association (NCEA).

Reverend Lawrence Cronin writes a column, "Good Ground," for *Catechist* magazine. The column focuses on the needs of the handicapped, offers suggestions, keeps readers abreast of the latest developments in legislation to aid the handicapped, reviews and recommends resource materials, and offers information about workshops and congresses. Father Cronin has also compiled an annotated bibliography, *Resources for Religious Education for Retarded People* (Arena Lettres).

Many dioceses have offices for special education and/or religious education for the handicapped.

Homebound Parishioners
Even though great efforts may be made to mainstream the handicapped into religious education programs, there will still be members of the community who, because of their disability, will be unable to participate. Home-visiting catechists should interview these students and their families to assess their needs and interests and help develop alternate programs to meet their needs.

Handicapped Catechists
Handicapped members of the community, depending upon the extent of their disability, should be encouraged to participate as teachers and assistants in religion programs. In many parishes the disabled are an untapped human resource.

HIGH SCHOOL PROGRAMS
Characteristic of adolescents during their high school years is their search for identity and their attempt to discover who they are apart from their parents and family. In the exploring process they wander away from close family

and neighborhood ties and from their customs and practices. They seek to put away the things of childhood, but also question what adulthood has in store for them.

This period is difficult for adolescents and their families. Many teaching catechists also find it difficult—especially when they see their favorite students from the elementary and junior high days move away from their former closeness to the church. Catechists involved with high school programs should keep the story of the Prodigal Son before them as a sign of hope.

Among the real and practical problems for the once-a-week religious education programs are the school, work and social schedules of most high school students. Many work part-time. They no longer go to a neighborhood school and, as a result, spend more time commuting each day. Their friends are drawn from a wider geographic area. They frequently have heavy after-school schedules.

Another typical problem is the attitude of some of these adolescents and their parents toward high school religious education. Many have lost the sense of urgency about religious instruction they had before all the "required" sacraments were received.

These problems raise questions for DREs and teaching catechists about maintaining contact and providing for the continued religious development of these young people. Parishes must re-examine—with students, parents and teachers—the assumptions they hold about religious education for high school students. They may find that many parents and students feel that enough instruction has been given. It is interesting that some researchers in the field of adolescent religious development call for more personal and involving religious *experiences* that go beyond instruction. Some basic practices and attitudes almost militate against developing strong programs for high school students. Elementary programs are easier to develop and staff, so some communities have concentrated their efforts and finances there where the responses are most visible. And, in a very human response, some adults in the community resent or give little credence to the adolescents' search for identity, their rebelliousness and their seeming lack of respect for community standards and practices. These adults assume the adolescents must "shape up" before they can be received by the community. Interestingly enough, however, the father in the Prodigal Son story did not set up criteria for his son's return.

As we noted in the essay *Adolescents*, this is a period critical to faith development, a time when young people begin to abandon the faith of their childhood or become more committed. Teachers must become conscious of the ways these students think, abstract, generalize, feel and question their worlds. The work of the catechetical team—and it might be noted that team ministry is also the thrust in adolescent religious education programs today—is to be present, to be available, to be resources to these questioning teens. The *NCD* makes an overwhelming demand on those working with youth:

> There seems to be no inherent reason why young people should become more prone to lose their faith as they grow older. They are exposed to competing world views and value systems, but catechesis can and should be adapted to mental age and to the social context and other circumstances (No. 200).

Unfortunately, the bulk of the text and journal material is still for the elementary level, but there certainly are enough resources available to provide parishes with some direction.

In 1977 the United States Catholic Conference, with the help of a grant from Our Sunday Visitor Inc., sponsored a symposium on the catechesis of children and youth. The report on the symposium, "Catechesis: Realities and Visions" (Publications Office, USCC) is a helpful resource for those involved with high school programs and youth ministries.

Some other readings for those working with high school students are *Crisis of Faith: The Religious Psychology of Adolescence* (Herder and Herder), *Five Cries of Youth* (Harper and Row), *Young Catholics in the United States and Canada* (Sadlier).

See also ADOLESCENTS, YOUTH MINISTRY and SEXUALITY.

HOLY DAYS AND HOLIDAYS

Holy days and holidays help us remember the past, celebrate the present and look forward hopefully to the future. The festivities of these days let us incorporate the joys and experiences of others into our own lives.

Many of the liturgical feasts of the Trinity, Christ and his mother renew our memories of what has been and the promise of what is to come. As we share in the saints' lives, we share in other human experiences of the Christian life. Nations and cultures celebrate holidays to recall their heroes, to remind themselves of struggles for independence, and to inspire them for days of future peace and solidarity.

Harvey Cox in *Feast of Fools* distinguishes man as "by his very nature a creature who not only works and thinks, but who sings, dances, prays, tells stories and celebrates." Holy days and holidays call us to celebrate.

These days are ideal for introducing the richness of the liturgical year, the history of various feasts and how they are celebrated. Going beyond the academic background and actually joining in celebration, however, is a superb classroom experience.

Many religion texts now provide lesson plans for special days such as Christmas, Epiphany, Easter and Pentecost. Some also include holidays like Halloween, Valentine's Day, Thanksgiving and Human Rights Day. Each program should discuss other possibilities that exist for celebration, for example, the parish patron's feast or a national holy day or holiday.

As part of their early planning for the year, teachers should survey their texts to see what lessons are offered for special days. Some texts put these supplementary lessons in the back of the book; others include them as part of the text. It is impossible for any text, however, to include every celebration day for each grade level.

Many teachers enjoy preparing their own holy day and holiday classes, often with the aid of supplementary books such as *Holy Days and Holidays* (Winston), *Doing, Dance and Drama* (Ave Maria Press) and *Liturgical Year in Puzzles* (Pflaum/Li). Some teachers celebrate the feast days of their students' patron saints. The students prepare celebrations based on an understanding and appreciation of the saints' lives.

A problem, frequently mentioned in this book, is that classes are not in session during the Christmas, Easter or Pentecost celebrations. Special efforts should be made to bring students together for liturgies and festivities to celebrate what they have learned and shared.

See also CELEBRATION, LITURGY and SAINTS.

HOLY ORDERS

The sacrament of holy orders used to be generally taught without qualifications because it was all so clear and precise. Men were ordained to the diaconate and priesthood and, with the exception of the Eastern uniate churches, were to remain celibate. Priests administered most of the sacraments, preached, distributed communion and exercised administrative and pastoral roles in the parish.

Catechesis for holy orders has changed, and the description of *orders* has become more subtle and requires refinement. Some new directions come from the strikingly visible changes of the last decades. The order of diaconate, formerly given only in connection with and on the way to priesthood, is now allowed to married men who are called to preach and baptize. Lay men and women are permitted to distribute the Eucharist, and the reading of the word of God is open to many of all ages.

The sharing of ministry and actions formerly restricted to priests has made it important for teacher-catechists to stress ordination to distinguish holy orders from other calls to service in the church. The *NCD* describes the work of those in *orders*—bishops, priests and deacons—as "proclaiming the word, embodying the gospel in the community of believers, leading the community in worship, healing its divisions and summoning its members to reconciliation" (No. 133).

In discussing ministry, religion texts usually distinguish the role of the ordained ministers and the call to service of other members of the Christian community.

Holy orders and related topics are usually introduced in the middle grades. At this age lessons on ministry can have a sense of remoteness and children may not be as interested and enthusiastic as some teaching catechists would like them to be. Young children are curious, however, about who does what in the sanctuary and why. Teaching catechists should take advantage of this natural curiosity and provide children with opportunities to meet with priests, deacons, lectors, cantors, eucharistic ministers and servers. Let them find out more about priesthood, ministry and orders through their questions and encounters. Children should have firsthand experiences through liturgies, prepared especially for them and with them. Weddings, baptisms, and anointings of the sick also provide children with opportunities to understand priestly ministry.

In today's world it is likely that teacher-catechists will be confronted by students with the question of the ordination of women. The best way to respond is with honesty about the state of the question today. Teachers should be informed about the church's stand on the question and also be aware of the groups within the church that are working for change of that position. Junior and senior high students may be aware of the level of controversy that exists from media coverage. If the topic comes up in class, it should not be covered up. Controversy is a healthy sign of a community willing to talk about its differences.

HOLY WEEK

Holy Week dramatically unveils the events leading to Easter. From Passion (Palm) Sunday to the Easter Vigil on Saturday night, the church invites us to reflect upon and remember these events and share in Christ's paschal mystery.

The Jewish passover meal offers a model of catechesis for Christian education. The youngest child at the meal asks the question, "Why is this night different from all other nights of the year?" The response, the Passover story, is given through the ritual meal and the many symbols and actions throughout the evening. Each year Christian children should be encouraged to ask the same question during Holy Week. Through the liturgies and lessons for each day the events of Holy Week should unfold and be celebrated.

Teacher-catechists often find some difficulty in communicating the special importance of Holy Week; many programs meet only once a week for instruction, and often that one class is cancelled. It is also difficult for students to learn about Holy Week through liturgies that are geared to adults. Young people must be prepared to understand and participate in the rich liturgies of this week.

Here are some practical suggestions. First, plan a calendar for catechetical programs and Holy Week liturgies with the joint cooperation of those involved. Use the classes during the week before and/or during Holy Week to introduce students to what will be going on and how they can participate.

Students of all age levels can be directly involved in the Palm Sunday procession and hosannas. Younger children should be prepared for the reading of the Passion by hearing a shorter version of it with an adapted vocabulary in class. Their attention should be called to this dramatic reading in church by telling them to listen carefully for parts of the story they are familiar with. Older students can prepare a gospel dramatization in class.

The events of Holy Thursday lend themselves to many classroom activities. Lessons about the Mass and its relationship to the Jewish Passover, seder meals, plays and skits about the Last Supper and the events of that night are but a few of the activities that teachers can use. Some parishes schedule a seder celebration for families sometime during the week.

A dramatization of the Way of the Cross prepared by the high school students for younger students is a popular parish activity for Good Friday. In some places classes organize outdoor stations of the cross with special prayers, poems, skits or music prepared for each station. A particular class (or family) can take the responsibility for preparing and setting up a cross or some other symbol of each station.

Students need help in appreciating the uniqueness of the Good Friday liturgy. Devote some class time to discussing and explaining the three-part service.

An important part of teaching Holy Week is to be sure that the lessons and activities don't build up to Good Friday without going beyond. Instruction must include the Easter Vigil and the church's invitation "to come together in vigil and prayer" on this "most holy night, when our Lord Jesus Christ passed from death to life." Classroom activities and lessons explaining the rich symbols of this night's liturgy—the Easter candle, the new fire and water—are needed. Renewing baptismal promises, making baptismal or Easter robes, designing paschal candles, choral readings of the Easter Proclamation (*Exultet*) and singing the Litany of the Saints can all be done in class to prepare for this night.

See also EASTER.

HOME CLASSES

Some teacher-catechists believe that home classes are the cure for all that is wrong with religious education. "The classroom boxes in and institutionalizes the presentation of religion" is a statement frequently heard in discussions about moving religion classes from the school to the teachers' homes.

The question of the best setting for religion classes is complex. On the positive side, many catechists who have taught in their homes appreciate the comfort, convenience and informality. They think the setting helps build teacher-student rapport and that children are more open to learning in the relaxed atmosphere of a private home after their long day in a classroom. Some express the idea that religion belongs in the home and should not be taught like a classroom subject.

Fewer restrictions encourage teachers to work on more activities and projects. Teachers report that attendance is better than in tradi-

tional classroom programs and that more families become involved. Large group get-togethers at the church or parish hall become more significant and special to the home-based students. Supervision by the DRE seems less formal in the home setting. And, in case of emergencies, canceling or extending classes is easier and more efficient.

On the negative side, some teacher-catechists find the home a distracting place filled with interruptions from the telephone and the doorbell. They prefer the classroom with its formality, structure and size. They find it hard to maintain discipline and keep the children's attention at home.

Audio-visual aids and other equipment are not as accessible and generally involve too much advance planning and transportation from the center. Students are more isolated because meetings and activities cannot be as easily shared with other groups. Liturgies for students and teachers may not be scheduled as frequently as when classes meet near the church.

Some teachers think that they receive less aid and attention from the DRE, the grade-level coordinator and other resource people simply because these people have difficulty visiting so many home classes. Catechists teaching at a centralized place are able to share ideas with each other more readily than those in the homes.

Both the positive and the negative aspects of the question provoke thought about optimum learning conditions and should be thoughtfully explored before decisions about class locations are made.

See also FACILITIES.

HOMEWORK

In religious education classes, especially those held once a week, homework must be interesting and meaningful in order to motivate students to want to do it and to remember to bring it back to class for discussion and review. Good teachers know that homework is effective if it is checked or read, commented on, evaluated and returned to the student.

Creative home assignments precipitate student interest and thinking and are often experiential. A good assignment introduces students into areas that they will usually investigate only when gently pushed or urged or given official permission to do so, for example, visit a church or hospital, interview a neighbor, watch a special television program or do library research.

Homework is a good means of individualizing instruction for students of different backgrounds, interests and talents. Homework geared to the special interests and skills of individuals can become an enriching experience for the entire class.

Frequently homework in an academic setting is used for grading or examination preparation. Teacher-catechists have to consider how homework is used in a religious education situation. Learning does not occur only during class time, and home assignments can extend the lessons and afford opportunities for their assimilation. Creative homework can be a challenge to teacher-catechists and their students.

See also CONTRACT LEARNING and BUSY-WORK AND GIMMICKS.

HOMILIES

The homily is a talk or discourse given by the priest or deacon on the readings of the day. The Liturgy of the Word is brought to completion and fruition by the homilist's words and the participants' reflections.

On some occasions, especially with small-group liturgies, the homilist opens the discourse by asking a question of the congregation or requesting comments on the readings of the day.

The teacher should prepare the students for the readings in advance of the liturgy. Younger students, especially, cannot absorb the meaning of the readings and homily after one hearing. For some liturgies, for Sunday or a special class liturgy, discuss the words and meanings of the readings after having them read aloud. Prepare students to take part in liturgical celebrations by helping them listen and recognize certain words and connect them to the themes of the seasons.

Homilists who spend time with the children in catechetical programs relate better to them during liturgies. Although it might be surprising, and perhaps disappointing, asking children about last Sunday's homily can be a revelation and a lesson in communication for the homilist.

A number of services for catechists and homilists are available for liturgical celebration and preparation. Some subscriptions offer ideas for classroom use (see PERIODICALS).

See also LITURGY.

I

IN-SERVICE TRAINING

In-service training, an ongoing process of helping catechists meet the challenge of teaching effectively, keeps a religious education program viable. The survey, *A National Inventory of Parish Catechetical Programs* (United States Catholic Conference), states that only a small number of parishes have all their teachers certified, indicating they have completed at least the basic catechist preparation courses. Most parishes find that their teacher-catechists range from professional religious educators to some last-minute volunteers whose preparation is minimal.

Continuing in-service educational opportunities must be developed by the parish with the assistance of the diocesan religious education office. Many Catholic colleges offer courses, workshops and seminars to assist in catechist formation.

The DRE should survey the teachers to determine individual needs in order to arrange various in-service programs for them. A record of each teacher's educational background should be kept in the religious education office.

These records must be kept current.

In-service training can be offered through seminars, lectures, courses, workshops, congresses, institutes, conventions, demonstrations and observations. Some assistance should be provided for problems that arise during the course of teaching.

Lectures can be one-shot attempts to keep teachers abreast of the latest developments in catechetics, or a series of talks on a theme of interest to any group of teachers, for example, a lecture series on sacramental theology for sacrament-preparation teachers.

Many dioceses provide courses, basic and advanced, for catechists. They usually offer courses in theology, liturgy, scripture, morality, educational psychology, catechetics and methodology. Some places offer advanced teaching certificates to catechists who complete these courses as part of their continuing education. Courses taken at local Catholic colleges are sometimes part of a degree program. Other offerings are for enrichment and growth.

Conventions, institutes and congresses, sponsored locally or nationally, offer teachers opportunities to explore areas of interest to them and to meet with catechists from other parishes and places to share ideas, problems and solutions. Most of these conventions have publishers' exhibits which show the latest religious education materials available.

Workshops provided as part of in-service assistance should be just that. The idea of a workshop implies doing. Workshops are most effective in methods courses when teachers are involved in doing demonstrations, working the audio-visual equipment, making art projects, etc.

The quality of in-service assistance is reflected in religious education programs. According to J. M. Lee, author of *Flow of Religious Instruction* (Pflaum), "Improved pedagogical skills far more than improved theological understanding is the key to more effective religion teaching now and in the years to come."

See also TEACHER PREPARATION AND TRAINING and LIBRARY AND RELIGIOUS EDUCATION RESOURCE ROOM.

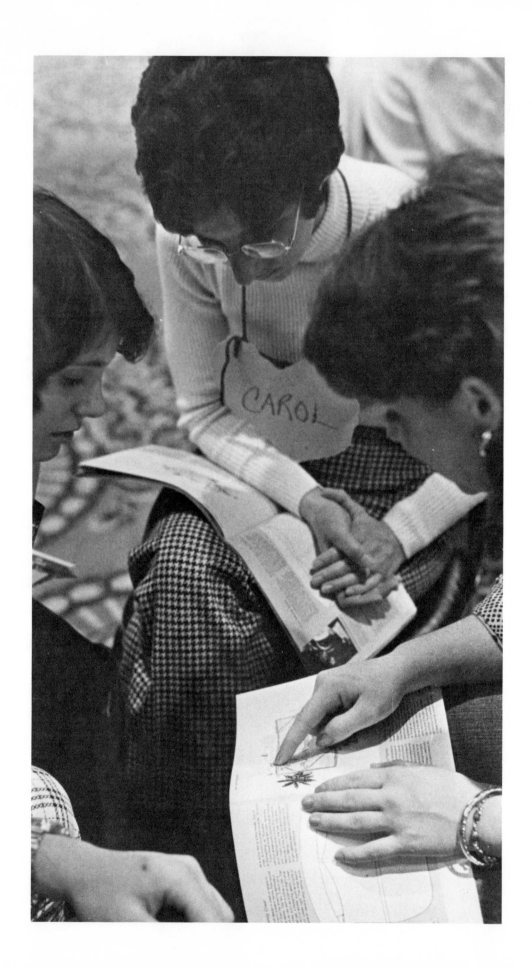

J

Journal
  (see DIARY)
JUNIOR HIGH SCHOOL PROGRAMS

K

Kindergarten Programs
  (see EARLY CHILDHOOD PROGRAMS)

Again he began to teach by the lakeside, but such a huge crowd gathered round him that he got into a boat on the lake and sat there. The people were all along the shore, at the water's edge. He taught them many things in parables (Mk 4:1-3).

J

JUNIOR HIGH SCHOOL PROGRAMS

Junior high schools were designed to provide a more guided and secure transition from the simpler elementary school life to the more complex world of high school. These years, usually grades seven through nine, have been considered so important that separate buildings and curriculum are the norm.

For parish religious education programs, these years have been the traditional confirmation years, with grades six, seven or eight generally used for the preparation and reception of the sacrament. As the junior high school was designed to help students move to the more adult world of high school, so too, confirmation classes seek to prepare young Christians for the adult life of the parish community.

Whether the program for this level is directed toward confirmation or is separated from sacramental preparation the problems encountered by teacher-catechists are considerable. The *NCD* goes so far as to indicate that for some preadolescents today, there can occur a crisis of faith, a term not formerly associated with this age level.

Educational psychologists have indicated that adolescence approaches earlier than at the turn of the century. Whereas 14 or 15 was probably closer to the average onset of adolescence, we now find the turbulent characteristics of puberty occurring earlier. The following descriptions of behavior are used by the *NCD* for preadolescence and puberty (10-13), the age for intermediate to junior high school programs.

‣ interests extend beyond the home to the peer group, which exercises an increasing influence on attitudes, values, and behavior.

‣ young people face the task of coming to terms with themselves and others as sexual beings.

‣ they need to accept themselves precisely as male or female and acquire a whole new way of relating to others.

‣ it involves some confusion, uncertainty, curiosity, awkwardness, and experimentation as they try on different patterns of behavior (No. 179).

Given this set of characteristics, catechesis for this age requires a curriculum, methodology and personnel adapted to these rapidly changing young people. Academic programs for these years take into account the relationship of a marked physical, emotional and intellectual change to school learning. Religious educators must also design catechetical programs which anticipate and ease such crises that arise in the young students as they move unevenly forward.

The junior high student is in a stage when hero-worship is popular and accepted by peers. The *NCD* suggests that teachers take the opportunity that this presents to offer the lives and deeds of saints and other outstanding persons, especially Jesus, as possible models.

Other suggestions for junior high school programs include the use of audiovisuals, projects, field trips, and activities that give students more responsibility. Community service, liturgical participation and social activities should all be a part of a junior high program.

A real aid for junior high teachers is *Designs in Affective Education: A Teacher Resource Program for Junior and Senior High* (Paulist Press).

See also CONFIRMATION, HIGH SCHOOL PROGRAMS, ADOLESCENTS, YOUTH MINISTRY and SEXUALITY.

L

Paul and Barnabas, however, stayed on in Antioch, and there with many others they taught and proclaimed the Good News, the word of the Lord (Acts 15:35).

L

LEARNING THEORY

How do we learn? It is a question fundamental to any teacher-preparation program and one that is not answered simply. Most educational psychologists agree that learning refers to a complex process that results in a relatively permanent change in behavior. They differ in their responses, however, about what constitutes this process.

At one major teacher-preparation center, Brooklyn College, students of education become involved in field-based courses, experiencing and observing the learning process by being with learners. These college observers begin to reflect on some of the components of learning: goals, directions, motivations, feelings, rewards, repetition, review, conditioning, relationships, intellect, environment, competition, subject matter, presentations and past experiences. The students begin to understand the process of learning by reflecting on their own experiences as learners and their observations of other learners. It is an excellent teacher-training and in-service model that can be applied to the training of teacher-catechists.

Psychologists attempt to answer the question of how human beings learn by offering various theories. Three of the major schools of thought—behaviorism, humanism and cognitive psychology—have offered practical insights to teachers.

Behaviorists believe that learning is an observable change in behavior. They hold that desired results for the learner can be effected through carefully worked out programs of positive and negative reinforcers. Behavior is modified by reinforcing desirable actions or skills and following undesirable behavior with no reinforcement (extinction) or in some cases with punishment.

The goals of behaviorists are skill mastery and learning competencies. In their teacher-centered approach the learner plays a relatively passive role. Rote learning, skill mastery of subject matter, and competencies are characteristics of behaviorism. B.F. Skinner is the psychologist most commonly associated with this approach.

Teacher-catechists observing students will recognize the following as applications of this theory: rote memorization of prayers; questions with memorized answers; reward systems for good behavior, attendance, doing homework and classroom participation. Stories which emphasize goodness rewarded and evil punished reinforce the behaviorist approach.

Humanists propose that learning must be meaningful and only occurs when the learner's intellect and emotions are involved. The social dimensions of learning are considered critical, and the humanists focus on the relationship between the teacher and learners, the learner's relationship with peers, and the learner's feelings about self. The individual needs of the students and the satisfaction of these needs are key concerns.

The teacher is a facilitator, that is, one who assists rather than directs. Active participation is encouraged since humanists stress learning by doing and the goals in learning are self-fulfillment and understanding. A leading proponent of this approach is Carl Rogers. Louis Raths and Sidney Simon's values-clarification process is a humanist methodology.

Religion teachers influenced by the humanists attempt to make religion meaningful to students, work to develop the learner's self-image and peer relationships, assist students in gaining insight and understanding and work to form community.

Cognitive psychologists approach learning as information processing, problem solving, and discovery. The learner sees or perceives relationships between ideas and a restructuring of thoughts and perceptions takes place. The emphasis is on the thought processes, not observable behavior. As new relationships and mental connections are perceived, the learner becomes able to apply these new perceptions in solving different problems and reaching new levels of understanding. The goals here are development of cognitive functions and the use of intelligence and insight.

An understanding of the learner's developmental level is critical to the teacher who serves as guide in the learner's exploration and discovery. Jean Piaget is a well-known cognitive psychologist whose contributions to the field of human development and moral thinking continue to have a major effect on teaching and parenting. Lawrence Kohlberg's moral-growth theory is of the cognitive school of thought.

Teacher-catechists will be able to recognize the influence of cognitive psychology in religious education. Many of the texts used today structure the content in meaningful units with built-in feedback opportunities. Lesson activities that promote participation, social interaction, problem solving and discovery are all applications of cognitive psychologists' theories.

In practice, there is no such thing as an exclusively behavioristic or humanistic teacher, or one who implements only the theories of the cognitive psychologists. Most learning situations contain elements of each theory. Each approach contributes to the overall structure of learning, and particular aspects of each theory have proved successful for particular objectives and goals.

See DEVELOPMENTAL PSYCHOLOGY, EDUCATIONAL PSYCHOLOGY, MOTIVATION, EXPERIENTIAL APPROACH and DIARY.

LECTURE METHOD

"Don't give me a big lecture about it." This is a common statement by teens to any adult seemingly on the verge of a long reprimand or wordy warning. Some young people associate *lecture* with preachiness, but it actually derives from a word meaning "to read" and implies a prepared script.

Often a lecturer does become preachy or long and boring, but that does not justify eliminating this method altogether from religious education. A well-prepared lecture presented by an enthusiastic person who is sensitive to and aware of the needs of the group can offer a superb learning experience. The method is a form of expository teaching in which the teacher presents material in a fully organized fashion to the students. It is designed to transmit a large amount of information to a group in a relatively short time. It is efficient, but has been criticized for placing students in too passive a role.

The advantages of a well-planned lecture, however, encourage teacher-catechists to use the method for introducing new material, ideas or information. It is a method geared more to students in the upper elementary grades and beyond.

Any teacher deciding to use the lecture method should note the ten commandments for a good lecturer:

YOU SHALL

I be well-prepared.

II be organized, specific and clear.

III not mumble, singsong or speak in a monotone.

IV always use vocabulary geared to the audience; beware of using "ten-dollar words," trying to impress or talking down to the group.

V be dramatic and enthusiastic for your audience's sake.

VI honor and respect each person before you.

VII remember to use humor and examples whenever you can.

VIII never go beyond the time for your lecture, even if the group begs you to do so.

IX be prepared to summarize as frequently as necessary to convey your message.

X remember that you are not the only expert in the field and leave some points for other experts to make.

LENT

Lent is an annual renewal of Christian conversion that prepares us for Easter. We teach most effectively about Lent by involving students in the ideas and practices called for by this season of action and change.

Lent begins with the visible signing with ashes and the command, "Repent and believe the good news." Students and teachers join together for the change of heart and mind that characterizes repentance. Lenten catechesis helps us pray, study and do good works that lead us restored and renewed to the celebration of our new lives at Easter. Lenten liturgies and classes invite us to change our lives. This change or *metanoia* takes place when people have experienced the Lord and want to share the experience.

Teaching catechists can prepare students to be open to the experience by familiarizing students with the good news they are asked to believe. The gospel readings for Lent, the stories that Jesus told about forgiveness, sinners repenting and returning to the Father, and the stories of the saints who changed their own lives offer a wealth of ideas for classes during the Lenten season.

Children learn from models. Many adults today acquired their attitudes about Lent from a community that publicly fasted and abstained and gave up things like smoking or movies during Lent. The changes that have taken place in recent years do not eliminate the sacrificial aspects of Lent. The church has asked people to personalize and interiorize sacrifice and conversion, however. Some teaching catechists feel this new emphasis erases the external practices of the past and as a result shy away from dealing with Lenten practices in the classroom.

For children, however, many of these customs and practices are ideal for communicating the meaning of change, renewal, conversion, repentance and sacrifice. Teachers, parents and all members of the adult community need to understand what children absorb from them. The signing with ashes becomes more meaningful to children when their experience during Lent is one of a community that is trying to change, to do better, to do more for others.

Children may need some of those concrete, external practices we frequently associate with past Lents. The mite box, the stations of the cross, the numerous ways of counting good deeds, the sacrifices for the poor and needy, the practices that fostered self-control ("giving up" and "offering up") are still good training exercises for Easter. Lessons about the changing seasons, the seed that dies to become a plant, the transformation of the caterpillar to a butterfly, the hatching egg and other transformations in nature ready young children for stories of the Easter mystery. All these customs, practices and lessons should help children go from the concrete to the abstract, from the external to the internal, according to their developmental ability.

As children mature they need help in working out more internal and personal responses in terms of prayer, meditation and service. Using the desert experiences of Moses, John the Baptizer and Jesus as models may help prepare them for action. Lent is a good time to retreat and junior and senior high school students appreciate some time to be together, to reflect and share.

Some classroom resources for Lent include: *The Way of the Cross* (Twenty-Third Publications), a filmstrip for junior and senior high school students that develops themes for Lent.

The Children of Light (ROA) filmstrip set Episode 9, "Lent," and Episode 10, "Easter," include a guide and spirit-master activities that are geared to children from kindergarten to about the third grade.

Simplification of Life Style, Nutrition, The Politics of Hunger and *Internal Trade Barriers* (Mass Media, The World Food Series) are all filmstrips that can be appropriately used for adult programs during Lent.

See also HOLY WEEK and EASTER.

LESSON PLANS

Good lesson plans, both long-range and immediate, are basic to good teaching. Long-range plans help teachers see the course as a whole; immediate plans help teachers with the lesson for the day.

Long-range planning starts with a calendar, a schedule of classes for the semester and the scope of the material to be taught. Special seasonal lessons and free days are noted. The number of lessons in each unit must be related to the number of class sessions. Meeting with other grade-level teachers helps determine what will be essential for each class, and what can be varied, combined or omitted.

From this beginning survey teachers can situate themselves and see the direction and purpose of the course. They can then make decisions about materials, supplies and equipment and tentatively schedule group activities, projects, liturgies, field trips and socials. Sacramental-preparation teachers must make note of scheduled reception dates and plan lessons accordingly.

Teacher's manuals provide lesson plans for each lesson. These must be adapted to student needs, time allotment, materials available and the individual teacher's abilities, talents and judgments. Whether using a lesson plan from a manual or an individually designed one, teachers should always write out their plans. This can be done on an index card or a piece of paper using key phrases to remind the teacher of sequence, content and method of the lesson. This is part of the immediate planning.

The following is an outline for an immediate lesson plan:

▸ topic, subject or theme
▸ aim (goals and objectives)
▸ material and equipment needed
▸ method or methods
▸ procedure
▸ summary
▸ preview of the next lesson

Lessons are never taught in isolation. They are related to past lessons and to those that follow. Lessons must always be seen as part of a larger whole, especially when classes meet only once a week. This main theme, for example, may be baptism. The *topic* for the day relates to the general subject or topic in a very specific way; for example, a lesson about God's family.

Knowing the theme of the lesson helps the teacher focus on a specific *aim* or objective. Teacher's manuals provide specific aims for each lesson. For teachers working without a manual, time and effort are required to establish, with care and precision, the purpose and object of the lesson. The goals of a lesson begin to evolve as the teacher reviews the material and tries to highlight key points.

Once an aim is clearly established and stated, it is easier to decide what *materials and equipment* will be needed. Audio-visual equipment and materials, art supplies, pencils, books, and so forth, should be checked for availability before the rest of the lesson is planned. Time for setting up equipment or obtaining supplies should be scheduled. As a lesson is being planned, ideas begin to surface for a variety of presentations and the teacher can choose the materials that will be most effective for the students.

An hour class period may involve several approaches to the theme. *Methods* should be selected by appropriateness to the grade level and to the topic of the lesson. A variety of methods should be used to maintain student interest and involvement. Many of the current texts suggest experiential lesson approaches that actively involve the students in the lesson.

A lesson, like a good story, has to have a beginning, middle and end. In planning the *procedure*, the sequence of the lesson from beginning to the end is outlined along with an approximate time allotted for each segment of the lesson. Teachers should note everything that is to be done—attendance, announcements, prayers, experiences, presentations, bathroom visit, snack, homework, etc. Included in this procedural planning should be time for summaries, conclusions and previews.

A *summary* helps students focus on the main points of the lesson, organize the material in their own minds and reinforce what has been learned. It is an important part of the lesson and should not be relegated to a few quick words by the teacher competing with the sounds of dismissal in the halls.

The lesson should not conclude with a summary but with a *preview* of the next lesson or session. The preview should be interesting enough to grab the students' attention, arouse their curiosity and warrant their return to class in anticipation of the next session. Advertisers use previews of coming attractions effectively. Teachers should utilize some of their previewing methods. To do this well, teachers need to have the overview of the course that long-range planning provides.

After each class, teachers should do a brief evaluation—what was successful, what didn't work out, what wasn't completed, how something was received by the students, their general response to the lesson, any of their insightful comments and anything that has to be remembered for the next lesson (see DIARY).

See also MANUALS FOR TEACHERS, AUDIO-VISUAL MATERIALS, ART PROJECTS AND ACTIVITIES and METHODS.

LIBRARY AND RELIGIOUS EDUCATION RESOURCE ROOM

More than half of the parishes responding to the survey for *A National Inventory of Parish Catechetical Programs* (United States Catholic Conference) have no parish library. The same survey, however, indicates that most catechetical programs have resource rooms or at least some space for educational hardware such as slide, movie and overhead projectors, tape recorders and record players.

A great asset for the entire parish, especially teaching catechists, is a good library. For some parishes it is the only place people have access to books on liturgy, doctrine, morality, catechetics, church history and scripture. Most parish libraries also include religious pamphlets and periodicals, reading lists for special interests and copies of the diocesan papers.

Periodicals for catechists and liturgists should be available to assist teachers in lesson preparation. Copies of religious education texts other than those used in the parish program should be in the library for supplementary lesson suggestions.

The library and resource room can be one and the same facility, or they can be separate rooms. The resource room should include instructional and learning materials for religion that can be borrowed by the teachers or other members of the parish for adult and family catechesis. Posters, charts, slides, films, filmstrips, pictures, records, tapes, prints, photographs and any other resources the parish owns can be organized for easy access and use.

Any discussion of a religious education library or resource room raises the question of accessibility. The value of any facility lies in how useful it is to the population it is intended to serve. Religious education libraries that are open only during school hours, or once or twice a week when religion classes meet, serve only a small segment of the parish population. Weekends and evenings, after parish liturgies, before, during and after classes are some of the optimum times to have the facilities available for use. Of course staffing for such a range of time must be considered. Many parishes attempt to make their library resources available to more people by recruiting volunteer catechists to serve as librarians, resource coordinators and assistants.

To make materials and equipment from the diocesan center more available, resource lists and bibliographies should be posted in the library. Also, a list of volunteers who are willing to pick up and deliver materials between the diocesan center and the parish should be posted.

Many parishes that have a Catholic school and a religious education program for public and other private-school students sometimes tend to duplicate religious education resources unnecessarily. A more extensive facility can be operated within the same budget if representatives of various parish groups communicate their needs and also share what they have.

The book, *Cataloging Made Easy: How to Organize Your Congregation's Library* (Seabury Press) is especially helpful to volunteers organizing a parish library.

LITURGY

Catechists teach about the Mass, the sacraments, the liturgical year, ritual, celebration, and the relationship between liturgy and life. As a result they also discover that they are involved in dealing with students' attitudes and feelings about liturgy. Teachers soon become aware of students who find Sunday Mass boring. Students tell of their annoyance and impatience with unwittingly finding themselves at a baptism during a Sunday parish liturgy, of their resistance to receiving the sacrament of reconciliation. They air their complaints about homilies.

The *Directory for Masses with Children* (Sacred Congregation for Divine Worship) offers some insights into the problem.

> Even in daily life children cannot always understand everything that they experience with adults, and they easily become weary. It cannot be expected, moreover, that everything in the liturgy will always be intelligible to them. Nonetheless, we may fear spiritual harm if over the years children repeatedly experience in the Church things that are scarcely comprehensible to them: recent psychological study has established how

profoundly children are formed by the religious experience of infancy and early childhood, according to their individual religious capacity (Introduction).

Not being able to relate to everything in the liturgy discourages some young people from participating at all. Teacher-catechists can be of great assistance in helping students relate to and understand liturgy through classroom experiences which will connect them to liturgical celebrations. Lessons that focus on meaning, symbols, rite and celebration should be presented according to the level of the group.

Younger children should be encouraged to learn prayers and songs that can help them join in the community's celebrations. Teachers should prepare them to look for things that are familiar to them, to listen to gospel stories, and to learn the gestures.

This preparation for at least partial participation can be extended among older students by discussing readings and liturgical themes in advance, and by relating the readings to class activities and projects. Some class projects can actually be used as part of the liturgy itself: making posters, banners and other thematic displays; preparing gospel dramatizations, readings, intercessions, music or dance; participating in the recessional, entrance or offering of the gifts.

Classes can prepare their own liturgy on occasion. The *Directory for Masses with Children* differentiates between "Masses with Adults in Which Children Also Participate" (Chapter 2) and "Masses with Children in Which Only a Few Adults Participate" (Chapter 3). Teachers preparing the latter will find adaptations in the *Directory* which encourage the participation of as many children as possible.

Publications such as *Celebration* (NCR Press) have a children's column that offers suggestions to help incorporate children into Sunday and holy day liturgies. *Catechist* (Peter Li) and *Religion Teacher's Journal* (Twenty-Third Publications) have the Sunday readings for each month listed along with suggestions for classroom activities.

All teaching catechists are also involved in sacramental catechesis. The *NCD* states that "sacramental catechesis has traditionally been of two kinds: preparation for the initial

celebration of the sacraments and continued enrichment following their first reception" (No. 36).

Preparation for the initial reception of particular sacraments is not as difficult for the teacher as continued enrichment. Children in preparation classes are usually more enthusiastic and responsive because the lessons are for a limited time and build up to the actual reception of the sacrament. Also, most of the themes are being presented for the first time.

Teachers involved with ongoing developmental lessons on the sacraments should carefully study the curriculum the students had for their first preparation and the sacramental instruction they have had since. Scope and sequence charts are of some help here. Care should be taken to avoid any semblance of the "same old thing."

Many texts use life experiences in teaching the sacraments. Lessons on the Eucharist call for the sharing of a meal, a celebration and community experience. Lessons about reconciliation include everyday apology situations in the school yard or lunch room, making up for offenses, and trying to be peacemakers at home and in school. Confirmation preparation includes service commitments to the community.

As students become more aware of the cycles in nature, the seasons, and the repeated celebrations in life, birthdays and anniversaries, the concept of liturgical year can be introduced. Younger children become familiar with liturgical feasts that they can relate to in some way, such as Christmas and Epiphany. As they mature, they make the connection between the life of Christ and his saints and the liturgical seasons more readily.

Religious calendars, made by the students or distributed by the parish or the local funeral home, are good visual aids for showing children the flow of the seasonal feasts.

A set of six filmstrips, *Naming the Days: the Liturgical Year* (Our Sunday Visitor), offers a good presentation of the idea of the liturgical year.

See also CELEBRATION and HOLY DAYS AND HOLIDAYS.

M

Mainstreaming
  (see HANDICAPPED)
MANUALS FOR TEACHERS
MATRIMONY
MEMORIZATION
METHODS
MORAL DEVELOPMENT
MORALITY
MOTIVATION
MUSIC

"Teacher, what must I do to inherit everlasting life?" *(Lk 10:25, NAB).*

M

MANUALS FOR TEACHERS

Most publishers of student texts for religious education also publish teacher's manuals to assist teachers in lesson preparation. Some are teacher's editions which include the student text and the manual in one volume. Others are books separate from the student text.

Each teacher should have a manual. Sharing them is not a good way to cut costs. Teachers should acquire the manuals well in advance of the beginning of classes, and those teachers who usually teach the same class from year to year should be allowed to keep the manual.

New teachers should be introduced to the manual and the text by an experienced teacher and not simply handed one with a comment like "this is all you need to teach with."

Teaching catechists should be encouraged to use the manual as a guide, adapting lessons and projects to the students in a particular course. Manuals are designed as an aid, not a crutch. For example, a teacher who uses the manual verbatim in class is using it as a crutch. For a personalized lesson plan, prepare with the manual before class and then write key words on index cards and refer to them during the actual lesson.

A good manual includes:

▸ a scope and sequence chart of the entire series to help teachers see their course in relationship to the rest of the program

▸ some theological background information

▸ a developmental profile of the youth for which the particular course has been designed

▸ an overview of lessons to be taught each week or session

▸ detailed lesson plans offering suggestions for methods and materials

Some manuals also include the following additional aids:

▸ a glossary of terms

▸ a bibliography for teachers, parents and students

▸ lists of resources and publishers

▸ optional lessons for special days

Anyone involved in text selection should give serious attention to the quality of the teacher's manual.

See also LESSON PLANS.

MATRIMONY

The *NCD* encourages parishes to provide programs for all married people which "foster supportive interaction between spouses and among couples" (No. 131). The Marriage Encounter movement is one of the programs that offer this kind of support to married couples.

Catechesis for preparation for the sacrament of matrimony is found primarily in programs for young adults, usually in the Cana and Pre-Cana type programs sponsored by the diocese and organized on the regional or parish level.

Marriage preparation courses have also been included in senior high religion classes. The *Directory* suggests that married couples be involved in this catechesis to high school students whenever and wherever possible.

Elementary level texts introduce the sacrament of matrimony in the middle grades. Prior to these lessons, primary grade students receive some readiness through stories and lessons about family life, and about being part of God's family. Instruction about matrimony at this elementary level often includes models the children are familiar with, namely their parents, relatives and neighbors who are married.

Because of the dramatic changes in American family life in recent years, teaching catechists must always be aware of and sensitive to the family situations of students. They should be cautious to teach the church's ideals without condemning people—it is quite possible that the parents of some of the students in a class have not attained these goals. One very upset fifth-grader left religion class with the fear that her parents were going to "burn in hell forever."

A teacher who is insecure or unsure of

how to handle a sensitive topic in marriage and family life should seek help and follow the lesson plan in the teacher's manual. Such precautions will help prevent the teacher from making remarks that frighten students or give them the wrong information.

Human sexuality should also be included in the curriculum on matrimony. Programs must be prepared to help students of all developmental levels understand their own sexuality and be ready for that aspect of catechesis for matrimony.

Matrimony, along with sexuality, has been generally treated as a moral issue. Both topics have not been given a continuing place in religious education. Perhaps the only lessons some young children receive about matrimony are based on stories of the Holy Family and the Wedding Feast of Cana.

Given the complexity of family life today, catechesis needs to consider integrating the church's concerns for married life, sexuality and spirituality with the best thinking offered by the social and behavioral studies.

MEMORIZATION

Memory enables people to carry within themselves their own tradition. A key person in many African tribes was a *griot*, or oral historian. In the earliest years of the church, the tradition was passed on by this very same process.

In this day of electronic information storage and retrieval, it is hard to understand such a method of passing on a culture. However, memory still has a role in education. The *NCD* affirms its role in catechetics:

> While catechesis cannot be limited to the repetition of formulas and it is essential that formulas and facts pertaining to the faith be understood, memorization has nevertheless had a special place in the handing-on of the faith throughout the ages and should continue to have such a place today, especially in catechetical programs for the young (No. 176e).

Pope John Paul II in his Apostolic Exhortation, *On Catechesis in Our Time*, recalls the various insights about memorization that were discussed at the 1977 synod. He points out cer-

tain disadvantages, "not in the least of which is that it lends itself to insufficient or at times nonexistent assimilation, reducing all knowledge to formulas that are repeated without being properly understood."

Many educators proposed that the excessive insistence in the past on committing catechism answers to memory was a good reason to abandon any use of memorization in religious education today. They pointed out that the pupils should not be asked to learn anything by rote if they do not understand it.

Many educational psychologists believe that memory plays a key role in learning. Perhaps in the past memorization was seen as an end in itself rather than a part of the complex process of learning. Learning theorist Robert Gagné suggests that there are eight separate phases in the process of converting information to learned knowledge. Three of these are related to memory—coding information for storage, retaining, and then recalling the material.

Teaching catechists must see the role of memory in relationship to the whole process of learning. Memorization definitely has a place in religious education. The *NCD* guidelines are helpful in understanding this role:

> "It should be adapted to the level and ability of the child and introduced in a gradual manner, through a process, which, begun early, continues gradually, flexibly, and never slavishly." It is through memorization that ". . . certain elements of Catholic faith, tradition, and practice are learned for a lifetime and can contribute to the individual's continued growth in understanding and living the faith" (No. 176e).

METHODS

A method is a *thoughtful* approach used to direct or induce learning, generally consisting of selected steps, ideas or movements that are guides for both teachers and students (method: from *meta odos*, Greek, "way towards").

The *NCD* notes especially two general approaches to learning, *inductive* and *deductive*. Through the inductive method teachers help students form general principles and conclusions based on their own experiences. For example, students are encouraged to remember and relate something about a friendship they have with someone; from these examples the learners can move to the concept of love.

Through the deductive method the students study the concept of love, through readings and discussions, and then look at where it specifically occurs in their own life experiences.

The inductive approach is closely associated with the more contemporary term "experiential learning," and the *NCD* endorses this general methodology as most helpful to students.

There are, however, many possible methods that are helpful to students. The choice of method must be based on its appropriateness to the age level, the culture, the size of the group, the time allotment, the subject and the abilities of the learners. Pope John Paul II has called for catechists to adopt different methods and has commented that the variety of methods used in catechetics is a sign of life for the believing community.

Teachers can choose from a variety of methods now in use in religious education: expository, lecture, discussion, discovery, problem solving, question-and-answer, open classroom, programmed learning, electronic instruction, and a wide range of experiential approaches. Audio-visual and electronic materials provide numerous opportunities for teachers to innovate with traditional learning approaches.

Underlying the choices of methods and materials is the basic overall aim of the religious education program. Catechists today are called to help develop Christians who are prepared to freely choose their faith and relate it to the world. This aim calls for a classroom methodology that gives students norms and traditions to consider, that helps young minds in the process of abstraction and generalization, and aids them as they examine their own worlds and prepare to integrate their beliefs and experiences.

MORAL DEVELOPMENT

In the past children were often viewed and treated as miniature adults. Today there is more understanding of the growth process from infancy through the stages leading to maturity.

The work of psychologist Jean Piaget in cognitive and moral development has generated much research in the areas of religious thinking, and moral judgment and development. *Judgment and Reasoning in the Child* (Littlefield, Adams and Co.) and the *Moral Judgment of the Child* (The Free Press) are among his many contributions to this field.

It is interesting to note that conscience is a traditional concept among moral theologians. The word is derived from the Latin "to know," and its use implies knowing within one's self. It requires cognitive thinking and acting (or not acting) based on knowledge. Included in discussions about morality are expressions that convey a process, and terms like *conscience formation* and *age of reason* imply developmental stages of human growth. Piaget compares moral stages of development with stages of cognitive growth.

Piaget describes what he calls moral judgment. In his work he analyzed how children at different stages of development evaluate a behavior described in a story. The verbal evaluations of the children who heard these stories correspond to the actual decisions made by children at the same developmental level in real-life situations. Piaget stresses there is no magic age when people become morally mature but that moral reasoning is a gradual process that develops in age-related stages.

Lawrence Kohlberg is a leading current spokesman for the view of moral development originated by Piaget. He holds that moral development occurs in an invariant sequence, with each stage qualitatively different from the preceding stage. Kohlberg describes how moral reasoning develops in a child and characterizes the stages of moral growth into adulthood.

For teacher-catechists, study of moral development provides insights into the traditional problems encountered in teaching morality to children.

Some resources for teacher-catechists: *Moral Development: A Guide to Piaget and Kohlberg* and *Value/Moral Education: Schools and Teachers* (Paulist Press); and an excellent work for guided study selections, *Toward Moral and Religious Maturity* (Silver Burdett Company).

See also MORALITY, DEVELOPMENTAL PSYCHOLOGY, COMMANDMENTS, BEATITUDES and RECONCILIATION.

MORALITY

The sign of commitment to Jesus is that his followers love one another. Jesus gave instruction and set examples of what this love entails, and his words and his way have become the basis for Christian morality.

Each age has had to learn to apply the words of Jesus. In the *NCD's* words, there is a moral response "not only to perennial challenges and temptations but to those which are typically contemporary" (No. 105).

In the New Testament, Christ aimed his harshest words at those who made morality an exclusively internal, self-centered code that ignored the needs of others. This temptation to make morality individual and rigid has been present throughout the church's history. Calls to reform and renew keep Jesus' way of life ever present as a model. The Second Vatican Council (1962-66) was a call to the church to re-examine its understanding of God's relationship to his people, to renew the spirit of the gospel message of peace, justice and love.

Catechetical materials, developed in accordance with recommendations of Vatican II, offer a wealth of ideas and insights into moral questions. These materials are geared to the levels of moral development of students.

The *NCD* comments extensively on morality today and should be used as a major curriculum resource outline (Part H: The Moral Life). In it teacher-catechists will find a more explicit call to "peace and justice, locally, nationally, and internationally." The document also presents contemporary issues that are of key concern to all people, especially

teachers; for example, "genocide, euthanasia, indiscriminate acts of war," and a more frank and explicit discussion of sexuality, the use of drugs and tobacco.

As a result of a wide range of exposure to the mass media, today's students encounter a range of values and differing points of view on questions of morality.

Simple answers and lists of do's and don'ts are not the solution for students and teachers exploring moral questions. Solid training and adequate resources are needed if catechists are to help students evaluate situations and distinguish morally right acts from those that are not.

See also BEATITUDES, COMMANDMENTS, MORAL DEVELOPMENT, RECONCILIATION and SIN.

MOTIVATION

In common usage, motivation refers to an incentive or an inducement to act. In educational psychology, motivation is a complex set of inner and outer drives that prompts students to move actively into the learning process, and that gets students to determine and act on goals. Educational theorists, such as Jerome Bruner and Abraham Maslow, have developed ideas on important human motives for learning.

Bruner speaks of motivation or the "will to learn" as part of human nature and intrinsic to learners. Intrinsic motivation is characterized by curiosity, the drive to achieve, and the need to work with others. In explaining motivation Bruner discusses curiosity as a powerful force that needs to be accepted, encouraged and disciplined in order to be effective. The drive to achieve competency is helpful where students feel comfortable and capable. Intrinsic motivation works best when there is some assurance of success. Reciprocity or working with others provides the stimulus to be part of a group process and to learn from others.

Two excellent works by Bruner, *The Process of Education* (Harvard University Press) and *Toward a Theory of Instruction* (Harvard University Press), provide teachers with some understanding of one of the most complex of all educational questions: How students get started and why they might resist.

Abraham Maslow's book, *Motivation and Personality* (Harper and Row), is a good library resource. According to Maslow, we are all driven to act in order to satisfy physiological, emotional and cognitive needs. He suggests a hierarchy of needs with two levels: deficiency needs and growth needs.

The deficiency needs are those rock-bottom aspects of human existence that must be satisfied before anything else can happen, before human beings can grow. These needs are physiological (food, rest, etc.), safety (physical and psychological), and love and esteem (sense of worth). When a person's deficiency needs are met, motivation is to growth. Growth needs are self-actualization, a desire to know and understand, and an appreciation of an aesthetic view of reality.

Maslow points out that we need to understand human development at each level before we can hope to motivate students to learn. Beginning a class with a good opener is not sufficient motivation. The needs of the students, their stage of development, and the significance of what is being taught, determine motivation. A teacher's concern for the comfort and safety of students, for establishing classroom structure and routine, for providing meaningful work, for treating the students with respect, and for motivating them to learn, are the really great "openers."

See DEVELOPMENTAL PSYCHOLOGY, EDUCATIONAL PSYCHOLOGY and LEARNING THEORY.

MUSIC

If catechetics is about Christians *who celebrate* then we need more and better music in our programs today. It is strange that people who plan music for weddings, cheer at games—and know thousands of tunes from commercials—don't miss music and song in religion classes.

Some people seem to assume that religious learning is too serious and music, if used at all, should be for the primary grade students. Religious educators have to see that music is an integral part of learning and celebrating. Children in school sing about their country, the alphabet, and number combinations. They learn many things through musical games and stories told in song. We have all reflected about love, friendship, grief and hope as we listened to and sang songs. And yet we often fail to use music as a means to communicate and teach the good news.

There are signs of improvement. More singing and instrumental music are used at most eucharistic celebrations. And most of the elementary and middle grade texts incorporate music in the lessons. There are some related problems, however. We rarely prepare children in once-a-week religion programs to sing with the community in church. Yet this is an excellent way to involve young people in the adult celebration of the liturgy. Another problem many teaching catechists confront when attempting to use music in class is the lack of equipment and materials. Too often part-time programs don't have access to a piano or organ, or do not have enough records, record players, tape recorders or song sheets.

Every religion class should include music in some form. A great help to many programs is the "floating" music teacher who can help prepare individual or combined classes for special liturgies, teach seasonal hymns, or help teachers develop music lessons. Children love to sing, and they need help in learning the words and being comfortable with the melody. Once children learn a song, they want every opportunity to be heard. Perhaps holding on to some of the customs and practices of the past, such as children's choirs, Christmas caroling, and Easter concerts, would help. Children should also be encouraged to play their instruments in class and for liturgies.

Some selected recordings:
The record components for many of the textbook series; *Pockets, Songs for the Journey* and *Take All the Lost Home* (Pastoral Arts Associates); *Songs for Young Children* (Paulist Press); *Close Your Eyes, Run, Come, See* and

Show Me Your Smile (F.E.L.); *You Are Invited, Ave Maria* (World Library Publications); *You Are My Friends* and *Reach for the Rainbow* (North American Liturgy Resources). Some Hispanic songbooks and recordings published by World Library Publications are worth noting—the songbook *Gloria al Señor* and Lucien Deiss' recordings *Gloria al Señor I* and *Gloria al Señor II*.

Some resource books: *Signs, Songs and Stories* (The Liturgical Conference) and *Let the Children Sing* (Seabury Press).

See also DANCE.

N

NAMES

NATIONAL CATECHETICAL DIRECTORY
  (NCD)

New Testament
  (see BIBLE)

O

Old Testament
  (see BIBLE)

OPEN CLASSROOM

Overview
  (see CURRICULUM;
       MANUALS FOR TEACHERS;
       LESSON PLANS)

"Now at last they know
that all you have given me comes indeed from you;
for I have given them
the teaching you gave to me
and they have truly accepted this, that I came from you,
and have believed that it was you who sent me" (Jn 17:7-8).

N

NAMES

Names are very personal. Teachers must observe caution, care and sensitivity in how they use students' names. They must find out the correct pronunciation of each full name, which can be done by having students introduce themselves. Some students prefer that a certain name be used in class. Teachers should inquire about this, note it in their roll book and make an effort to use the preferred name or nickname.

Teachers should clearly write their own name on the board and then pronounce it for the class. This helps students to remember who their teachers are, especially young students in a once-a-week class. It helps them feel more secure and comfortable in class.

A sign of the teacher's respect and concern is the ability to remember who the students are and to call them by name. This takes a deliberate effort for those teaching only once a week. For the first few classes, it may be necessary to use name cards, some type of seating chart or other helpful devices. We know some primary teachers who take a class picture the first day of class and print the students' names on it as a getting-to-know-you activity. The frequent use of student names in class helps each member of the class learn who the others are and it fosters community.

The ability to call a student by name also helps maintain order and discipline. When students realize that you know who they are, they are less inclined to try to get away with something. Discipline begins with the knowledge that both teachers and students have good communication.

Students' names should never be used in any slighting or joking manner, nor should any reference be made in an offensive way about an ethnic origin or personality trait.

NATIONAL CATECHETICAL DIRECTORY (NCD)

Throughout this book we quote the *National Catechetical Directory (NCD)*. Its full title is *Sharing the Light of Faith: National Catechetical Directory for Catholics of the United States,* a document approved in November of 1977 by the National Conference of Catholic Bishops.

This is a major pioneer work and unlike any previous American document on catechetics. The Third Plenary Council of Baltimore (1884) had issued a definitive policy statement on Catholic education for parish schools, endorsing the *Baltimore Catechism* for religious education. In the 1930s the bishops of the United States enlisted support for the Confraternity of Christian Doctrine. But nowhere in American church documents do we find what the *NCD* offers now: a comprehensive overview with guidelines, suggestions, norms and resources based upon a broad consensus of theologians, educators, scholars, parents and catechists.

This directory is a response to a 1971 Vatican *General Catechetical Directory (GCD)* which gave general principles governing catechetical activities in the universal church and requiring the development of national directories. The national directories were given "the task of filling out this outline and applying it to the circumstances of individual countries and regions." (In the United States a helpful work appeared, *Catechetics in Context* (Our Sunday Visitor Press), which offered the entire *General Catechetical Directory* with notes and commentary by Father Berard Marthaler, O.F.M. Conv.)

The *NCD* was developed over a period of five years of consultation, review and revision. At one point at least 60,000 draft copies were circulated throughout the country for feedback.

The fruit of these efforts has been generally well accepted. The *NCD* text, on the whole, is interesting, effectively organized and comprehensive. Theoretical points are made in clear language and practical examples given. The book is well illustrated and designed, with an excellent table of contents and index. Unfortunately, there is no adequate bibliography.

The *National Catechetical Directory* must and can be read by anyone involved in catechetics. Study groups and teacher-preparation courses could easily use sections for discussion. Most Catholic bookstores and diocesan offices of religious education carry the *NCD*. Much of the work is evident in the topics in this handbook.

O

OPEN CLASSROOM

Open classroom is not a term commonly used in religious education but it is a concept that can be applied.

Open classroom refers to the creation of an environment that encourages student-initiated learning. It is also referred to as informal education; it is characterized by flexible space, time and instruction. Students are encouraged to work at their own pace, choosing activities and topics that interest them. The teacher attempts to individualize the instruction.

A catechist teaching religion once a week might attempt setting up a modified open classroom once a month or every six weeks. Advance scheduling notices must be sent home if this session goes beyond set class hours or is on a different day. All the teachers for a given grade level can prepare the open classroom.

If several teachers are involved, they can use several classrooms, the auditorium or the gym. If only one is preparing an open-classroom day, learning centers, quiet corners and activity stations can be set up in the room. The theme the class is studying is expressed in some way at each location. Children are free to choose what they would like to do and to shift from one activity or place to another. The students should be involved in setting up the learning centers. At times during the course of the session or day a teacher may conduct an activity for the entire group, but most of the planning is geared to interaction among the students and between students and teacher.

More concretely, a fifth grade working with sacramental lessons could set up the following learning stations:

▶ filmstrips on sacraments

▶ slides of some member of the group's reception of a sacrament

▶ a table with puzzles and quiz sheets about the sacraments

▶ a library corner with books related to the theme

▶ a table set up with art supplies for students to use in expressing something they learned

▶ a drama corner where students can prepare skits or dramatizations of the rites of particular sacraments

▶ a question box; a priest can be invited for a talk or to answer questions in the box

▶ a tape cassette with a prepared lesson to listen to or some blank tapes for students to record related songs, prayers or readings

▶ a record player with records of music used for liturgies

During this time teachers circulate to assist individual children and talk to them about what they have chosen to do. Aides are of great assistance.

Educators use the open classroom for all subject areas taught in school. The religion teacher can use it to assist children in experiencing many activities related to the major themes taught.

See also EXPERIENTIAL APPROACH and PLAY.

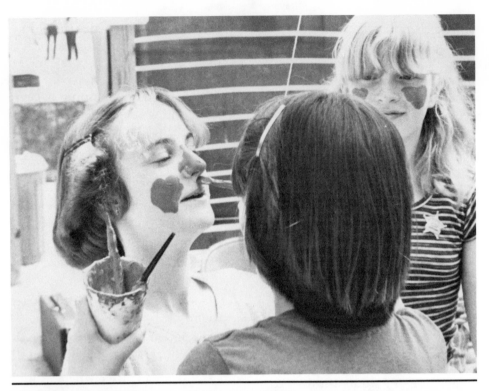

P

PARALITURGY

Penance
  (see RECONCILIATION)

PENTECOST

PERIODICALS

PLAY

PRAYER

Preschool Programs
  (see EARLY CHILDHOOD PROGRAMS)

PROGRAM EVALUATION

Q

QUESTION-AND-ANSWER METHOD

The apostles rejoined Jesus and told him all they had done and taught. Then he said to them, "You must come away to some lonely place all by yourselves and rest for a while" (Mk 6:30-31).

P

PARALITURGY

A paraliturgy takes the format and some of the elements of a liturgy and modifies them. They are not liturgies, nor are they substitutes for them. Sometimes paraliturgies are called bible vigils, prayer meetings or scripture services. Usually, they are developed for special occasions and celebrations or based on a particular theme. According to the *NCD*, paraliturgies:

> . . . can deepen faith, strengthen community, foster Christian love, lead to more ardent and fruitful participation in sacramental celebration and intensify the community's commitment to social justice. They offer opportunities for broad participation in planning and leadership. Catechists can foster appreciation of scriptural prayer by planning paraliturgies with those they catechize and providing frequent opportunities for such prayer (No. 142).

Participants in a paraliturgy are encouraged to adapt it to their own free expression, their own needs to celebrate and share prayer. Students should be encouraged to bring something of themselves into the celebration—a talent, a reading, a prayer, or an expression of an art form, such as a simple dance or pantomime.

A teacher can adapt a paraliturgy to the developmental level of the students, helping them select themes from the curriculum, from sacramental-preparation material or a holy day, holiday or church season. Appropriate readings from scripture and other sources should be selected which would precipitate some reflection, meditation and concentration on a theme and how it relates to the lives and understanding of the participants. Hymns, songs or other musical expressions should be incorporated, along with time for quiet reflection, prepared or spontaneous prayers. Audiovisuals are frequently used.

Paraliturgies for elementary students should be short, active and involving. Junior and senior high school students enjoy preparing their own forms and like to include some time for sharing ideas and thoughts and for socializing.

Paraliturgies can be celebrated in the church, chapel, classroom, on the school playground, in a park, a home or any place that is practical and comfortable.

See also LITURGY, CELEBRATION, HOLY DAYS AND HOLIDAYS and PRAYER.

PENTECOST

Pentecost poses a practical problem for teacher-catechists. It is a movable feast, celebrated 50 days after Easter, usually in late May or early June. In many parishes religion classes or programs have ended, and summer bible or vacation schools have not yet begun.

The religion texts that most frequently present lessons on Pentecost are those developed for confirmation preparation and are used at any time of the year that the sacrament is to be administered. Few other texts have lesson plans for Pentecost since publishers tend to follow the school year in their scope and sequence.

This raises the question of whether or not religious education should be slavishly following a school calendar instead of a liturgical calendar which would give Pentecost its rightful emphasis and attention in religious education programs.

If, however, the religious education program is coming to the end of its "year" just as Pentecost is approaching, here are some practical suggestions.

1) Prepare the music, readings, a dance or special activity for a Pentecost liturgy with the class before the program ends. Arrange for a special meeting just before Pentecost to review the preparation and then have a celebration.

2) Since Pentecost is the birthday of the church, teacher-catechists could suggest and participate with their students in a birthday party with the parish community. This is an appropriate occasion for celebrating community and making catechetical efforts in forming community (see CATECHESIS).

3) Have students prepare some bulletin suggestions for the week before Pentecost that foster awareness of the feast.

4) Have a group prepare a dramatic account of the descent of the Holy Spirit. High school students can use tape recorders and multimedia material to make a good sanctuary presentation.

5) Schedule a Pentecost gathering for students and plan activities that capture the experience of the first Pentecost gathering, that is, the coming of the Spirit, the receiving of the gifts, listening to Peter's preaching, and the feeling of community.

6) Prepare symbols of Pentecost to be explained and displayed during the liturgies. Caution: Some of the symbols that are quite clear to older students and adults are far removed from the world of the younger child.

See also EASTER.

PERIODICALS

A number of good periodicals are available to religious educators. The following provide teacher-catechists with a wide variety of background information, current research, practical suggestions, in-service assistance, book reviews, and resources for all areas of catechesis.

Catechetics on the Move (Twenty-Third Publications, P.O. Box 180, W. Mystic, CT 06388. Ten times a year.)

Catechetics on the Move features articles about new trends, in-service training ideas, workshop plans, ideas from DREs in the field, reviews of materials, information about upcoming events of interest to religious educators, and interviews with people in various catechetical ministries. Subscribers can send a self-addressed envelope for bonuses such as elementary text evaluations, high school text reviews, a catechist's covenant ceremony, etc.

It is published in a format which allows it to be kept in a binder which can be purchased with a subscription.

Catechist (Peter Li, Inc., 2451 E. River Road, Dayton, OH 45439. Eight times during the school year.)

Emphasizing religious education for professionals and volunteer catechists, this magazine offers practical and readable materials, how-to articles, seasonal suggestions for classroom use, ideas for liturgical expression, information on college programs and congresses that are of interest to catechists, suggestions on methods, and reviews of available material. Certain suggestions are laid out for duplication by subscribers, such as art outlines, puzzles, games and scripts for plays.

Celebration (National Catholic Reporter Publishing Company, P.O. Box 281, Kansas City, MO 64141.)

A creative worship service primarily for parishes, this publication can be of great assistance to catechists. It offers homily suggestions, scripture background for the liturgical readings, a resource service for subscribers providing discount prices for recent publications, a monthly newsletter, and columns for planning liturgies. There is a separate children's column with notes for involving children in activities before, during and after celebrations; and puzzles and activities that can be used at home or in the classroom to relate the Sunday readings and themes to the interest level of the children. *Celebration* offers packets for each Sunday and major holy days in the month.

Film and Broadcasting Review (U.S. Catholic Conference, 1011 First Ave., New York, NY 10022. Twice a month.)

This review provides religious educators with features on theatre, television and media broadcasting, resource information, and reviews of current and classic films. It is an excellent religious education library resource for teachers.

The Living Light (W. H. Sadlier, Inc., 11 Park Place, New York, NY 10007. Quarterly.)

This is the official publication of the Department of Education of the United States Catholic Conference. It "provides a forum for catechists and professional educators, designed to present developments and trends, to identify problems and issues, to report on research, to encourage critical thinking and to contribute to decision-making in the field of religious education and pastoral action." It is published in collaboration with members of the Department of Religion and Religious Education at the Catholic University of America in Washington, D.C.

Mass Media Newsletter (Twenty-Third Publications, P.O. Box 180, W. Mystic, CT 06388. Twenty times a year.)

Films that can be rented from Mass Media Ministries are summarized and graded for interest level. Suggestions are sometimes given for use in religious education. Synopses and ratings are given for current films. Attention is called to television specials and programs that are of interest to educators. Articles appear enough in advance for teachers to order seasonal films or arrange for group viewing of a television program as a home assignment.

Modern Ministries (Grace Publishing, 1201 E. David Rd., Dayton, OH 45429. Nine times a year.)

For catechists in all areas of ministry, including religious education. Articles deal with liturgy, youth ministry, service to the aged, teacher as minister, peace education, family ministry, parish renewal, and approaches to evangelization.

Modern Liturgy (Resource Publications, Box 444, Saratoga, CA 95070. Eight times a year.)

The publisher provides: (a) a full community subscription which includes *Modern Liturgy* magazine reprint license, plus four stereo cassettes, or (b) individual subscriptions to the magazine alone for eight issues. Articles are historical, theological, and practical, including sample or model services, and liturgical art forms for use in worship and/or religious education classes.

PACE (St. Mary's College Press, Terrace Heights, Winona, MN 55987.)

PACE (Professional Approaches for Christian Educators) is a multipurpose tool for religious educators, especially diocesan and parish directors. The loose-leaf format of *PACE* is designed for subscribers who receive permission to reproduce articles they wish to distribute to teachers and parishes. Subscribers receive binders which are divided by categories such as teacher training, adult education, discussion groups, staff training, parish councils, college religious studies programs, etc. Topics in *PACE* include theology, scripture, ethics, education, program materials, methods.

Religion Teacher's Journal (Twenty-Third Publications, P.O. Box 180, W. Mystic, CT 06388. Eight times during the school year.)

Directed to both professional and volunteer teachers of religion, this magazine offers ideas for the liturgical season, tips for teaching, theological updates, creative class projects, reviews of books and the latest multimedia materials.

Religious Education (Religious Education Association, 409 Prospect St., New Haven, CT 06510. Bimonthly.)

The official publication of the Religious Education Association of the United States and Canada, an interfaith organization, this scholarly journal "seeks to present, on an adequate scientific plane, those factors which make for improvement in religious and moral education." Subscription is usually through membership in the Association, but individual issues can be obtained.

Today's Catholic Teacher (Peter Li, Inc., 2451 E. River Rd., Dayton, OH 45439. Eight times during the school year.)

The value of this magazine for religion teachers lies in many of the articles on classroom management, individualization, pedagogy in general, plus a good number of articles specifically directed to religion and religious education themes.

Today's Parish (Twenty-Third Publications, P.O. Box 180, W. Mystic, CT 06388. Eight times during the school year.)

Articles on parish programs, liturgy, family projects and suggestions for pastoral ministry are but a few of the many themes interesting to catechists. Recent publications in liturgy and ministry are reviewed monthly.

PLAY

On the first day of school, a kindergarten teacher announced, "Now you will begin to come to work each day, just like Mommy and Daddy; you are in kindergarten and there's no more time for just play."

That statement was enough to have the parents of a little girl, who was very enthusiastic about going to school, ask the principal to place their daughter with another teacher.

Drastic? Not if you consider that a teacher's whole philosophy can be expressed in a statement like that. And considering what we know of play from Plato to Piaget, that kindergarten teacher was on the wrong path for learning.

Play is an important part of learning, growing and developing. In his *Republic*, Plato focused on the important nature of child's play, "avoid compulsion and let early education be a manner of amusement . . . children learn by games; compulsory education cannot remain in the soul."

Many parents and teachers unfortunately still do not see play as a positive aspect of growth and development. They feel it is a waste of time and something a child will grow out of.

"The assumption that children at play are not learning anything valuable—not developing or being prepared for school life—is distressingly widespread. It couldn't be more wrong," according to Piers and Landau, in their book *The Gift of Play* (Walker and Company).

Play is a necessary component for development of imagination and creativity. Professor Nina Lieberman of Brooklyn College has done extensive studies on play. In her book, *Playfulness, Its Relationship to Imagination and Creativity*, she talks about the concept of playfulness:

> The lightheartedness that we find as a quality of play essential to imagination and creativity . . . is a behavior that goes beyond the childhood years. And this activity, through its component parts of a sense of humor, manifest joy and spontaneity, has major implications for childrearing practices, educational planning, career choices and leisure pursuits.

Professor Lieberman adds, "playfulness survives play and becomes a personality trait of the individual."

For catechists, play is a way to help children learn, develop self-confidence and begin to form the sense of belonging which is a prerequisite to forming community. Teachers need to provide opportunities for both structured and spontaneous play. That comes more easily with the utilization of experiential techniques, of hands-on work, of group projects, or group play. The *NCD* advises catechists to "provide appropriate experiences" at each level, and play is most suitable for the young.

Play, fantasy and imagination are real assets and tools of the young mind. A way to involve children in learning is to let them "play" out events, persons, situations. In *Doing, Dance & Drama* (Ave Maria Press) we attempt to capture the spirit of play and communicate it to teachers with some concrete suggestions. A major concern of catechists is not to lose the sense of play and imagination that students bring to class.

See EXPERIENTIAL APPROACH.

PRAYER

The apostles saw Jesus at prayer and were moved to ask him to teach them how to pray. Children will also want to pray if they see positive examples of people praying at home, in church and in class. Teaching catechists will find that the best way to teach prayer is by praying with the students.

Lessons in the primary grades center around the relationship children have with God, how he loves and cares for them. Prayer must be taught in terms of this loving relationship—as a communication with God.

Children gradually come to understand the need for communication in any relationship they have—with their parents, their best friend, their teachers and classmates. They also learn from experience that there are many ways of communicating with someone. Some of these ways are quite formal, others spontaneous; some communications are very private, while still others are more public or part of a group experience.

The children should become familiar with formal prayers as well as informal, spontaneous prayers. Through classroom prayer experiences they should begin to realize the difference between private and public prayer.

Children learn many of the formula prayers through the public repetition of them in church and in school. They love to memorize and do so quite readily. However, these prayers should not be sent home as an assignment to be memorized or written. (A friend's son came home recently with the assignment to write the Our Father 10 times.) There is no need to give deadlines or create tensions about learning a prayer. Children may learn the prayer in this manner, but they will not learn to pray.

Many teacher-catechists get a bit flustered when they hear some of their students' renditions of prayers, such as "Our Father, whose art's in heaven," "Hail Mary, full of grapes," or "I am hardly sorry for having defended you." If teachers carefully listen to children's versions of the Pledge of Allegiance or the *Star-Spangled Banner* they will hear similar patterns. Any time children memorize words that do not fully make sense to them they mimic what they hear, using the rhythm and rhyme of the piece. Should we, then, teach these formula prayers to young children? Saying the prayers in the presence of the children is all that is needed for them to begin to pick them up. By knowing the words, even their own rendition, the children feel like a part of the group that is praying. They become familiar with words before getting any formal lessons about meaning.

Teachers can help children connect with the prayers of the Mass by having them listen to, sing or dance the great Amen, the Our Father, or the Holy, Holy, Holy.

Children need help in understanding that private prayer is their own personal communication with God. Many teachers use students' own experiences of friendship as a starting point. Saying "hello," "nice to see you," "please help," "I'm sorry," "thank you," "I like you," "come to my party" to a friend,

or hearing these words, does something for a friendship. Some of these human expressions of friendship also capture what theologians refer to as petition, contrition and thanksgiving. Visits, sharing quiet times, discussions, and celebrations with people help foster friendships very much in the way a person's relationship with God intensifies through prayer.

Speaking of those entering adolescence, the *NCD* says:

> Private prayer tends to become more personal and reflective now, while ritualized prayer often loses its attraction.

The *NCD* goes on to say:

> Young people who see no point to prayer and meditation should be introduced—or reintroduced—to the idea that it is personal communication with Jesus and, through and in Him, with the Father (No. 180).

Interestingly enough, in today's society young people have become attracted to much of what Eastern religions have to offer in terms of meditation and reflection. Perhaps the rich tradition of the church's spiritual exercises and contemplative practices should be made known to young people who seem to search everywhere for "inner peace."

Jesus, the teacher, offers some advice about praying. "In your prayers do not babble as the pagans do, for they think that by using many words they will make themselves heard" (Mt 6:7). Teaching catechists should keep this in mind when they pray with their class.

In addition to the Bible, some teachers will find the following resources helpful: *Experiments in Prayer* and *The Bible Prayer Book* (Ave Maria Press), *Breakaway* (Argus Communications), and *Songs for the Journey* (Fountain House/PAA), a record of familiar prayers like the Our Father, Hail Mary, and some psalms.

See also LITURGY, CELEBRATION and PARALITURGY.

PROGRAM EVALUATION

All catechetical programs should be evaluated regularly in the light of established goals and objectives. Program planners and directors should provide built-in ways of getting feedback from participants, especially teacher-catechists, parents and students.

For most programs the key to evaluation will be regular staff and faculty meetings where open discussion is encouraged. The use of an advisory board is an additional means of providing continuing dialogue among administrators, teachers, parish leaders and program participants.

Formal instruments for evaluation have been devised by the United States Catholic Conference (USCC) and the National Catholic Educational Association (NCEA). Many parishes also use their own evaluation forms. Written evaluations can ask teacher-catechists to comment on some of the following:

▸ communication of the Christian message
▸ sense of community
▸ opportunities for service
▸ student liturgies
▸ textbooks
▸ teacher's manuals
▸ student response
▸ class schedules
▸ communications
▸ faculty meetings
▸ resources
▸ in-service assistance
▸ needs
▸ difficulties
▸ rewarding experiences
▸ teaching facilities
▸ parent involvement
▸ recommendations for the future

Meetings with parents should provide opportunities for them to offer some input into program planning and evaluation. Student participants are another source of evaluation. (Their attendance, of course, provides some statement of evaluation.) Students should be asked, depending upon their age level and ability, to respond in writing (preferably anonymously) with an evaluation of such things as community activities, liturgies, service projects, texts, class schedules, and field trips.

Any evaluation must be productive in order to encourage people to actively participate in the project. If program evaluations are seen as mechnical end-of-the-year rituals, people eventually refuse to participate in them. Evaluations are valuable only when the DRE takes the results seriously and when they are used for discussion and planning meetings with the staff and advisory board.

Q

QUESTION-AND-ANSWER METHOD

Some of us can still remember and quote numerous questions and exact answers from our catechism books. When we were students, if we answered with the exact wording of the catechism we "knew" our lesson. Some of us even remember an old game based on the *Baltimore Catechism*—one student gave the answer, the other had to give the question.

While there is a value in the question-and-answer approach and the memorization of material, problems arose when it was used to the exclusion of all other approaches. The emphasis on exact memorization of answers left little time for the enrichment of explanations and discussions.

Two important aspects of the question-and-answer approach are important to religious educators: the *use* of the question-and-answer method in class and the *technique* of good questioning.

Teaching catechists use questioning techniques to achieve the following objectives: to clarify students' thinking, to provoke discussion, to encourage broader participation, to enable quick review, and to precipitate student reflection.

Questions lead to various types of thinking. The type of question that is designed to elicit memorized facts, such as those discussed in the beginning of this essay, requires simple memory. Other questions require a broader thinking. For example, questions that have an expected response within a certain framework require convergent thinking. Those questions that encourage free and creative expression, where there is no one correct answer, require divergent thinking. Evaluative thinking is elicited by teachers who ask questions that deal with judgments, require decisions, clarify values or make comparisons.

Teachers must use all types of questions in order to foster various levels of thought among the students. Most experienced teachers know the value of preparing key questions in advance. Appropriate questions do not always automatically come to mind during the lesson, and some must be written out as part of the lesson plan.

For effective use of this method ask questions which

▸ have a specific purpose
▸ are clear and precise
▸ are suited to the level of the class

R

READING SKILLS
RECONCILIATION
REGISTRATION
RELEASED TIME
RESOURCE PEOPLE

"We know that you are a teacher who comes from God"
(Jn 3:2).

R

READING SKILLS

Religion textbooks are prepared with the intention of meeting a broad range of reading abilities in a particular grade level. Despite this attempt, teacher-catechists soon realize that the reading skills of students in one class can be broader than any text can encompass.

Religion classes are not meant to be reading classes, and texts should not be used as readers. The catechist should not teach using the text as *the* lesson, spending the entire class time having students read the text, line by line, paragraph after paragraph.

Many students are self-conscious about being asked to read in the presence of their peers because they are poor readers, or in some cases, non-readers. If a lesson calls for reading from the text, scripture or other source, teachers should ask for volunteers, and extend the courtesy of some advance notice, giving them time to at least skim the piece. This gives the students the opportunity to pick up the general thrust of the reading and to locate unfamiliar or difficult-to-pronounce words. Some teachers use a surprise call to read as a means of finding out "who's not paying attention." This is an unnecessary game for a teacher in tune with the class.

It is helpful to all students to pronounce and discuss words that are new to them or part of a specialized vocabulary at the beginning of the lesson. In other words, if the lesson includes terms that perhaps even the proficient readers may not have encountered in any other context, such as *testament, covenant, sacrament,* teachers should devise ways of helping the students assimilate the concept and add the word to their vocabularies.

In the early grades the better student texts are basically pictorial with little dependence on the written word. The words are in the teacher's manuals and parents' components. In middle grades the texts have more reading material, but suggestions in the teacher's manual help teachers plan lessons that incorporate the poorer readers into the lesson.

Courses for junior and senior high school students often involve independent reading assignments that provide material for class discussions. Teachers must plan introductions and build in summations that will assist students who have had difficulty with the reading.

RECONCILIATION

This letter, sent to parents in a large city parish, shows the practical relationships among catechists, parents and children.

> Preparing children for the sacrament of reconciliation at St. Thomas is a combined effort of parents, priests, and religion teachers. The role of parents in preparing their children for reconciliation began before the child started school and is a continuing theme in all homes.
>
> Parents, consciously and unconsciously, are instilling in their children a hierarchy of values, a sense of right and wrong, an understanding of the words (and more importantly the meaning) "I'm sorry," "apology," "forgiveness," "I won't do that again," and "I'll try harder." All of these concepts are fundamental in preparing for everyday life in our communities. They are also important in a child's preparation for the sacrament of reconciliation.
>
> Teachers in the classroom cannot replace parents as guides in this all-important development. In fact, it is impossible to teach a child in a classroom what "sorrow" really means if the child has never been forgiven, or perhaps never heard his father apologize to his mother. It is difficult to teach the moral code of honesty or "Thou shall not steal" in a classroom if another principle is used at home during income tax time or when selling a used car.
>
> In our program parents are asked to evaluate what they have done toward the moral development of their child. Where is the emphasis placed in terms of values? What is considered "good" or "bad" in the home? How are contrition and forgiveness expressed in the family?
>
> The following bible stories are related to sin and reconciliation.

> Mark 2:1-12   The Paralytic at Capharnaum
> Luke 15:2-7   Parable of the Lost Sheep
> Luke 7:36-50   The Penitent Woman in Simon's House
> John 4:1-45   The Woman at Jacob's Well
> Luke 15:11-32   Parable of the Prodigal Son

John 20:19-23   The Sharing in the Power to Forgive

1 Peter 2:20-25   Christ Died for Man's Sins

This letter is a plan for catechists and parents to assume correct roles in the work of forgiveness with young children, especially the ones who come to class once a week. The *NCD* states that catechesis for this sacrament must

> always respect the natural disposition, ability, age and circumstances of individuals. It seeks, first, to make clear the relationship of the sacrament to the child's life; second, to help the child recognize moral good and evil, repent of wrongdoing, and turn for forgiveness to Christ and the Church; third, to encourage the child to see that, in this sacrament, faith is expressed by being forgiven and forgiving; fourth, to encourage the child to approach the sacrament freely and regularly (No. 126).

Both the parish letter and the *NCD* remind catechists and parents that children learn from their own concrete experiences. It is from this experiential learning that young children are led to the appropriate celebration of reconciliation.

New directives provide everyone with the option of receiving the sacrament either face to face with a priest, or anonymously in a confessional. Although the options may be difficult to provide to an entire class, care must be exercised that students know from the very beginning that they have the right and privilege to choose whatever form they want.

The *NCD* directs that catechesis for reconciliation and first communion must be "kept distinct by a clear and unhurried separation" (No. 126). Young children cannot easily understand the Eucharist and reconciliation if preparation for the two is tied together closely in the traditional program of about 30 one-hour classes in second grade.

Catechists who study children's moral development, and who understand how children celebrate, are resource people for priests and parents in leading young children to a good beginning with this sacrament.

In the upper years of the catechetical program, reconciliation takes on fuller dimensions as students grow in moral awareness, and as the program helps them to see more clearly their responsibilities to themselves and others. Also as the junior and senior high school students become peer conscious, communal celebrations of reconciliation take on greater significance in their lives.

The change in name from confession or penance to reconciliation, and the changes in the rite itself, have given new meaning to this sacrament and made its reception less mechanical.

See also MORAL DEVELOPMENT, MORALITY, SIN, COMMANDMENTS, BEATITUDES and VALUES CLARIFICATION.

REGISTRATION

The practical reasons given for conducting a registration usually include: grouping students into classes; scheduling enough classes and reserving space; recruiting teachers; ordering textbooks and supplies; officially committing students to a program; collecting registration fees and/or book money; recording important information about program participants; and distributing handbooks.

Although some parishes see registration as a necessary procedure that can be reduced to the simple distribution of forms and collection of money, others feel it is a good opportunity to meet parents and students. For these parishes it is not just an administrative task of the DRE and a few volunteers. Teaching catechists also are invited to meet people, some orientation session is prepared, program materials displayed, parent materials distributed and some refreshments provided. People are encouraged to linger, chat and ask questions about the program.

Certain information taken at registration is helpful for teacher-catechists. Before classes begin, teachers should be given the opportunity to review the registration forms of their students. Class lists with students' names, addresses and phone numbers are usually prepared for each teacher. In addition to that information, teachers should know

▶ any special disability or illness that might require attention

▸ a parent or guardian's home and work phone numbers

▸ the phone number of a relative or friend who can be reached in case of an emergency

▸ the religious education background

▸ the sacraments received

▸ the child's birthday

▸ the siblings registered in the program

Any personal data collected should be treated as confidential and all teachers should be reminded of this at the time they are given access to registration information.

See also EMERGENCIES AND FIRST AID.

RELEASED TIME

One major catechetical problem is how to get enough time to teach Catholic students in public school about Jesus. We have a large and growing number of school-age children in the public education system where religion cannot be taught.

To handle this problem churches have generally conducted part-time, once-a-week Sunday or sabbath schools, or after-hours classes, totally separated from the regular school day.

Another method, a compromise by church and state over school time, is *released time*. In this system students are excused from public schools during regular sessions for one or more hours each week, at the request of their parents, to receive religious education at the church of their choosing.

In 1973, a United States Catholic Conference study found that approximately 22 states allowed this practice, but as a national religious instruction arrangement for Catholics, its usage is apparently minimal. It is popular in some centers, like New York City, Atlanta, Georgia, and parts of Minnesota and Michigan. But in most of the country, it is either not acceptable or not used.

The *NCD* (No. 235) makes note of released time, commenting on its advantages and problems. From the *NCD* source, the United States

Catholic Conference (USCC) study, and our experiences in New York City, we suggest considering the following:

Advantages

▸ Classes are offered during the regular learning hours, and children are not brought back for after-school sessions.

▸ Saturdays and Sundays are left free for family activities, and also other types of parish activities for children and adolescents.

▸ Clergy and lay people who might not be free during after-school hours, are frequently available to serve as teaching catechists at this time.

▸ In comparison with after-school, evening, and weekend programs, attendance tends to be stronger.

▸ It promotes public dialogue and cooperation between public schools and local churches.

Disadvantages

▸ If the Catholic school building is used, its students must be dismissed early on released-time day to make classrooms, and often faculty, available to public school students.

▸ Transportation must be arranged from the public school to the religious education site.

▸ Students may be tired and inattentive because of the trip from one school to another, and because religion is being taught at the end of a long day.

▸ Students must bring their texts to the public school first and then to religion classes. This is sometimes a problem for young children.

▸ Since few religious education released-time programs seem to go beyond elementary school, students accustomed to the practice of official time off for religion may drop out when they must go on their own.

▸ Released time of one or two hours a week makes religious education seem like a small and inadequate portion of the students' total school time; it appears to be a tag-on to the important learning of the regular school.

The American public school system with its exclusion of religion from education is a continuous source of concern to many Americans. An hour or two a week in the regular schedule of learning is not a solution to the need for comprehensive religious education, but the released-time concept needs to be known and studied for possible directions in the future.

RESOURCE PEOPLE

Inviting resource people or guest speakers to share ideas and offer insights to the group adds a new dimension. They can provide in-service opportunities for teachers or enrich the classroom experience for students.

The following resource people are valuable to teacher-catechists:

▸ Members of the diocesan or parish catechist-formation team.

▸ Publishers' representatives who will demonstrate the creative use of their religion-text series and other materials, and answer teachers' questions. Many publishers are willing to provide this service free of charge to parishes that plan to use or are using their materials.

▸ Members of the parish who have expertise in areas that might assist teachers, such as art, music, dance, drama, liturgy, special education and counselling.

▸ Master teachers who can demonstrate teaching techniques.

▸ The religious education librarian or person in charge of the resource room who can offer a workshop presenting new materials and offering suggestions for use of all equipment and materials.

Listed in alphabetical order are some of the many resource people and guest speakers who can be invited to meet with students in class.

▸ altar society member
▸ artist
▸ cana couple
▸ Catholic Charities worker or representative

▸ census taker (parish)
▸ choir director or member
▸ deacon
▸ Director of Religious Education (DRE)
▸ doctor
▸ drug and alcohol abuse expert
▸ eucharistic minister
▸ family (sponsoring refugees, involved in Christian Family Movement or family catechetics)
▸ foster parent
▸ inner-city worker
▸ lay missionary
▸ liturgist
▸ minister
▸ missionary
▸ musician
▸ nun
▸ nurse
▸ parish council member
▸ Peace Corps worker
▸ peace movement worker
▸ permanent deacon
▸ postulant from the parish
▸ priest from the parish or a neighboring one
▸ priest of another rite
▸ rabbi
▸ religious educator
▸ religious order member
▸ seminarian from the parish
▸ service organization member or representative (St. Vincent de Paul Society, Mt. Carmel Guild; Xavier Society for the Blind)
▸ sex educator
▸ social worker
▸ sodality member
▸ Third Order member (Franciscan, Dominican, Capuchin)
▸ usher (parish)
▸ volunteer service worker

Inviting guests to the classroom requires planning and imagination. Speakers should fit into the overall program and be cleared by the administration. Teacher-catechists should keep the theme of the course in mind when planning to invite outside speakers. These people should be told what the class has been studying and how you expect them to fit into the program. Resource people should be given specific information about the time of the session, what they are expected to do, the age range of the students, and what the students' needs are.

The class should be prepared for a guest speaker or special program; for example, the purpose of this person's visit, how long it will be, and what is expected from the class.

Religious education programs that use resource people usually do not invite guests more than once or twice a year for any class. Some of the high school elective courses, however, are planned around a series of guest speakers that offer various aspects of the same topic. For example, a course on marriage can include a priest, a married couple, an engaged couple, a doctor, a nurse, a family counsellor, a teacher-catechist and a psychologist.

S

SAINTS

Scheduling
   (see ADMINISTRATION;
        FACULTY MEETINGS;
        ELECTIVE COURSES;
        REGISTRATION)

Scope and Sequence
   (see CURRICULUM)

Scripture
   (see BIBLE)

SERVICE

SEXUALITY

SIN

Status of Catechists
   (see COMMISSIONING OF CATECHISTS)

SUBSTITUTES

SUPERVISION AND EVALUATION OF TEACHERS

Support Systems
   (see TEACHER PREPARATION AND TRAINING;
        COMMUNITY;
        GRADE-LEVEL COORDINATORS;
        VOLUNTEERS)

Jesus had now finished what he wanted to say, and his teaching made a deep impression on the people because he taught them with authority, and not like their own scribes (Mt 7:28-29).

S

SAINTS

In the past, reminders of the church's saints seemed more visible to the classroom teacher. Each grade had a patron saint for the year, stories of the saints were found in various textbooks, and pictures and statues of the saints decorated most classrooms.

Vatican II made great efforts to review the church's position on the saints. Historically, problems arose as fanciful stories and tall tales became interwoven with the solid tradition of people who led outstanding lives of holiness.

The review of saints by Vatican II resulted in the removal of several names, most of non-existent people, from the list of saints.

In addition the Council also eliminated several very real saints from the canon of the Mass in order to simplify that beautiful prayer. The liturgical calendar was also reorganized to restore the central emphasis on the paschal mystery that had been obscured by too many saints' feast days that seemed more important than feasts of our Lord.

For some people, all this revision seemed to lessen the glory and importance of saints in our church and in the classrooms. This is not the case.

The saints are the heroes of the church, and the church needs her heroes. Every generation has found the need for heroic persons who embody virtues, goals, and potentials, both for the individual and the whole community. Catechists know that good role models help students shape ideals, clarify values, and form attitudes. Saints are good role models and are also a way of teaching tradition and history. Great deeds and great thinking are most alive in the stories of other human beings. The humanness of a Matt Talbot or a Martin Luther King, the commitment of a Mother Teresa or the witness of a Dorothy Day are marvelous lessons about believing communities.

The Feast of All Saints, November 1, and the more secularized vigil, Halloween or the Eve of All Hallows, are appropriate times for teaching about and celebrating these heroes. Recounting their lives can be done through drama, the use of filmstrips, reading biographies, and storytelling. The liturgy for the day can be prepared by classes, and an All Saints' Day parade is a marvelous experience of our "saintly" history.

Lessons on baptism and confirmation offer other opportunities to remember saints as models and patrons.

Jesus told stories to help the people learn. Catechists will find a wealth of stories for lessons in the annals of the saints. Here are some resources we recommend:

Exciting stories of Christian heroes and heroines are told by Boniface Hanley, O.F.M., in the book, *Ten Christians* (Ave Maria Press).

The Saints Book by Kate Dooley (Paulist Press) tells stories about the better-known saints, both men and women.

A book for children of all ages is *The Saint Book for Parents, Teachers, Homilists, Storytellers and Children* by Mary Reed Newland (Seabury Press). It includes saints for every month of the year.

Stories about people not found on the usual lists can be found in two books by Leo Knowles, *Candidates for Sainthood* and *Saints Who Changed* (Carillon Books).

A color/sound filmstrip, *All Saints' Day* (Ikonographics) is a good film, especially for All Saints' Day. The theme centers around the variety of paths to holiness. *Lives of Saints* (Ikonographics) includes Patrick of Ireland, Francis of Assisi, Joan of Orleans and Therese of Lisieux. The interest level starts with fifth or sixth graders. *New World Saints* (Our Sunday Visitor Press) is a filmstrip for junior high and older students in which John Neumann, Frances Cabrini, Rose of Lima, Martin de Porres, Elizabeth Seton, and Peter Claver speak through dramatic narratives.

A lesson plan and directions for an All Saints' Day parade can be found in *Doing, Dance and Drama* by Jack and Arlene Wrigley Murphy (Ave Maria Press).

See also HOLY DAYS AND HOLIDAYS, CELEBRATION and LITURGY.

SERVICE

One of the four main objectives of any catechetical program is to motivate students and staff to service for others. Teaching catechists must be aware of and committed to this purpose. The sign of healthiness in any program will be its dedication to the idea that Jesus came "not to be served, but to serve" (Mt 20:28).

The *NCD* suggests to catechists that in the *early years* of religious training "efforts to instill a sense of mission and concern for others help lay a foundation for later service projects, as does study of the lives of saints and outstanding contemporaries" (No. 232).

Confirmation programs now have ". . . performance standards for Church membership and community service; requiring a specified minimum number of hours of service to qualify for Confirmation" (No. 119). To help develop lasting motivation for service to others, the *NCD* further suggests that part of youth programs should include "Service opportunities (e.g., visiting the aged or shut-ins, assisting catechists who teach handicapped children, (and) working with community action programs" (No. 228).

The call to service is not limited to individual actions or local projects only. It is also ". . . linked to efforts to achieve social justice and has been traditionally expressed in the spiritual and corporal works of mercy" (No. 32).

Care and planning are extremely important to the success and effectiveness of these activities. The same principles of organization, structure, and purpose utilized in lesson planning, field trips, or any group activity are required tools for service programs.

Some general observations:

▸ Any service activity must always be appropriate to the abilities, developmental levels, and schedules of the students and their families.

▸ At the elementary and secondary levels, adult supervision is needed with all community or school service work.

▸ Because good service requires skill and some talents, as well as good will, time should be given to screening and training students.

▸ Planning for the year should include the less frequently scheduled projects suitable for the young children, the sustained and continuous programs for junior and senior high school students, and any joint or parish-wide cooperative ventures.

▸ In larger parishes some coordination or clearing of individual class or grade-level projects within the program, and with other groups in the parish, might be necessary. As in the tradition of the diaconate in the early church, perhaps the present-day deacons or some other minister could supervise and assist with all the parish service activities.

▸ Tact, good judgment, and sensitivity toward those in need are paramount. Adults need to help students work out suitable approaches and directions for helping others.

SEXUALITY

Ever since the first woman and man discovered their own nakedness, the scriptures have recounted human struggles with questions about sex and sexuality. Many of the church's teachings and controversies have concerned sexual problems. The church fathers had difficulties with some aspects of human sexuality, but they also extolled sexual union and frequently used vivid bodily images in their descriptions of divine love.

Educators are finding themselves in the front line of a problem involving the continued calls for formal programs of instruction in human sexuality. The *NCD* has encouraged catechists to take an active part in providing such programs for students.

Current terminology stresses catechesis and education in "human sexuality" rather than "sex education." Developmental psychologists have helped us understand that in human development from infancy through old age, a person's sexual dimension is greater and more inclusive than genital activity alone. Human sexuality is integral to our growth as persons and as social beings.

There are aspects of sexuality that obviously include sexual expression in genital activity and social relationships. With these, educators are called upon to help people understand and accept their own sexual identities and develop positive attitudes toward sexuality.

In spite of efforts and concern, educators may find a reticence or an aversion regarding sexuality in our culture that is reflected in our language. The discomfort experienced by some attempting to use proper terminology indicates the depth of the problem.

Another problem faced is the controversy often found attached to introducing sex education or courses in sexuality. There are heated arguments on the rights of parents and suggestions of moral decline. The *NCD* advises parents to become acquainted with any proposals for education in sexuality and be involved in planning, presenting and evaluating such programs.

A major section of the *NCD* (No. 191) spells out in detail the types of programs that must be realized today. It follows mandates from Vatican II for a "positive and prudent sexual education," and from similar calls in the U.S. Bishops' documents, *Human Life Today* (1968) and *To Teach as Jesus Did* (1972). As a follow-up to these recommendations and the program suggestions of the *NCD*, the United States Catholic Conference (USCC) has published *Education in Human Sexuality for Christians; Guidelines for Discussion and Planning* (1981), a book for people responsible for planning and offering programs in human sexuality.

The *NCD* states that "Education in sexuality includes all dimensions of the topic: moral, spiritual, psychological, emotional and physical." The document goes on to stress that "Sexuality is an important element of the human personality, and an integral part of one's overall consciousness. It is both a central aspect of one's self-understanding (i.e., as male or female) and a crucial factor in one's relationships with others" (No. 191).

It is hoped that more programs will incorporate some catechesis for sexuality at all levels, using materials and methods appropriate to each community's needs. More on the topic is found in some high school text material, catechetical journals and scholarly works, but

grassroots support and implementation is somewhat lacking. Teacher-catechists, as well as parents, frequently need help in carefully establishing their own understanding of the meaning of human sexuality. Many anxieties, questions and problems must be brought into catechetical forums so that the mandates of Vatican II and the bishops can be actively implemented.

SIN

Many teacher-catechists express a certain confusion about topics such as mortal and venial sin and how they are presented in present-day catechetics. These teachers often point out the differences found in the catechism lessons of their childhood and the texts that are used today.

The *NCD* refers to the "lesser offense (venial sin)" and the "grave offense (mortal sin)." The grave offense is a radical disruption of a person's "relationship with the Father," whereas the lesser offense paves "the way for the commission of grave sins" (No. 98).

Children in religious education classes are introduced to the concept of sin only after they spend much time understanding the "relationship with the Father" that the *Directory* talks about. Lessons about family relationships and personal friendships, together with lessons about Jesus' special love for them, are all necessary before any young child can even *begin* to understand the complexity of sin. Sin is presented in terms of how these relationships are changed as a result of willful wrongdoing.

Primary grade children still think concretely. In presenting lessons on sin and forgiveness, most religion texts respect their inability to generalize. Children at this level make quantitative judgments more easily than qualitative ones. To many children of this age, accidentally dropping a stack of the family's best dishes is much worse than deliberately breaking one in anger. Time is spent in class telling stories and describing real-life situations that help children distinguish between mistakes and sin. Categorizing mortally sinful acts and those that are not does not accomplish anything with primary grade students.

Middle grade students are gradually introduced to lessons that deal with concepts of intentionality, degrees of seriousness, temptation, communal aspects of sin, and the human condition. Each topic is presented in a manner appropriate to the level of maturity of the group.

Junior and senior high students begin studies that help them realize that sin and its effects are present in people's own personal lives as well as in society. Some of the areas covered at this level, and in greater depth at the adult level, are mentioned in the *NCD* (No. 98):

▸ exploitative relationships

▸ loveless families

▸ unjust social structures and policies

▸ crimes by and against individuals and creation

▸ the oppression of the weak

▸ the manipulation of the vulnerable

▸ explosive tensions among nations and among ideological, racial and religious groups and classes

▸ the scandalous gulf between those who waste goods and resources, and those who live and die amid deprivation and underdevelopment

▸ wars and preparations for war

See also MORAL DEVELOPMENT, MORALITY, RECONCILIATION and DEVELOPMENTAL PSYCHOLOGY.

SUBSTITUTES

In the most perfect of all worlds teachers would never get sick, have an emergency, a personal problem, a family event, a bout with exhaustion or a dental appointment. But until that happens, anyone involved in scheduling teachers has the problem of recruiting and preparing substitutes.

To help reduce teacher absences, administrators should simply ask whether or not the candidate for teaching is *always free* on the day of class. A once-a-month doctor's appointment could become a major problem for some-one planning to teach once a week on that day.

Substitutes should be recruited in the same way and at the same time as teacher-catechists. They should participate in the teacher preparation courses and be given special assistance as substitute teachers.

A pool of substitutes should be created before classes begin, perhaps by setting up a rotating schedule of what weeks they will be "on call." More people volunteer to substitute if they realize that they do not have to be available every week and if they are assured of some preparation for and assistance with the task. Whatever the plan for substitutes may be, avoid getting caught with last-minute calls asking who's free and willing to teach.

An efficient way to prepare substitutes is by grade level. Primary, intermediate, junior and senior high school substitutes should familiarize themselves with the texts, materials and methods used at those levels. They can meet with teachers they are preparing to cover for to discuss basic procedures. Grade-level coordinators can be of great assistance to absentee teachers and their substitutes.

A teacher's absence is also a problem for students. Some students are used to having substitutes give them a free period or study time, or they see them as glorified babysitters. Classes that frequently need substitute teachers often have discipline problems and show a drop in attendance. Problems often occur with continuity, teacher-student rapport, and the students' sense of community. A teacher missing several classes has a disrupting effect on the whole teaching-learning process.

Some guidelines for teacher-catechists preparing for substitutes include:

▸ Give as much advance notice of your absence as possible.

▸ Leave a list of students' names and a seating chart.

▸ Prepare a lesson plan if time permits. Avoid leaving an abundance of unrelated, busy-work handouts.

▸ Leave the teacher's manual and student text with the lesson theme identified and page numbers given.

▸ Have the class routine written out in advance. Include procedures for attendance, homework check, bathroom visit, dismissal, fire drill, opening and closing activities.

▸ Inform the substitute of any planned activities that need special directions or equipment such as a party, play, liturgy, visit to church, film or an art project. Decide with the person substituting what must be postponed and what can be done that day.

▸ Make known any special student needs that may require the teacher's attention, such as a disability, an illness, a particular discipline problem, or a special dismissal arrangement.

In emergencies, the procedure for arranging for a substitute should be simple, but must include the following information:

▸ your name

▸ the grade you teach

▸ room number

▸ time of your class (if you are part of a large program)

▸ the lesson to be taught

SUPERVISION AND EVALUATION OF TEACHERS

Religious educators, even though they deal with many unmeasurable elements, generally profit from the assistance offered through supervision.

What do we mean by supervision? Our view is conveyed by the words of educator George Albert Coe, who thought the basic concept of supervision was "intimate sharing in burden-bearing." It is a continuing dialogue between teacher and supervisor that helps teachers look at their work in process. In some respects it is like a routine physical checkup that helps people evaluate how they are doing, what they can do to continue in good health, and what must be done to remedy any problems.

Each program needs a professional development plan that includes assistance dealing with classroom situations as they arise, formal and informal visits to the classroom, and help for teachers in the self-evaluating process. In programs staffed primarily by volunteers, there may be some normal resistance and fear of having a visitor. Perhaps the most important role of the DRE in this situation is to establish professionalism among teachers so that they see the need for help and are anxious to learn and share new approaches.

This type of professionalism comes from dialogue within programs about procedures, individual differences in teaching approaches, common goals, and ways to improve. Supervision and evaluation help teacher-catechists by the following: utilizing evaluative techniques, reviewing lesson-planning procedures, audio-taping lessons for playback and comments, using diaries, visiting among teachers who are free to observe.

Where the DRE considers it important for each teacher to be visited, some such routine procedures as the following should be worked out:

▸ establish a mutually convenient day and time for the visit

▸ decide on how long the visit will last and what approach the observer will take

▸ discuss the lesson for that class in advance

▸ allow adequate time, immediately after class or within a reasonable time, to talk over the session

▸ show teachers any written report before a final copy is filed

If a community spirit of sharing and growing together is fostered, most administrators and teachers will welcome the opportunity to better the religious education program.

Teachers themselves help supervisors by learning to think and reflect on their own work in class. From self-examinations good evaluation questions surface.

A check list for any teacher should include:

▸ Am I prepared and organized?
  Do I use methods appropriate for the age and developmental levels of my students?
  Do I make efforts to be interesting?

Do I take time to select the best materials and methods for each lesson?

▶ Do I follow my lesson plans?

Do I have the objectives in mind as I proceed with the lesson, or do I get lost?

Do I allow for flexibility in my plans?

Am I clear in presenting lessons and giving directions?

Do I start and finish class on time?

▶ What is my relationship with the students?

Do I enjoy what I am doing?

Do I know all the students by name?

Do I make the classroom a safe, comfortable and secure learning environment?

Do I provide opportunities for students to express themselves?

Do I listen?

Am I conscious of my appearance, my tone of voice, my body language when I am in class?

Do I have problems with discipline? How do I approach these?

Do the students know that I love them and care for them?

▶ What is my relationship to the program?

Am I absent unnecessarily?

Am I on time or, better yet, early?

Do I schedule time to talk with students or meet with colleagues?

Am I accurate and conscientious in keeping student records, attendance, grading, correcting and returning home assignments and tests?

Have I been able to read, attend a workshop, and share ideas with grade-level teachers?

See also TEACHER PREPARATION AND TRAINING, LESSON PLANS, FACULTY MEETINGS and MANUALS FOR TEACHERS.

T

TEACHER PREPARATION AND TRAINING
TEAM TEACHING
TEXTBOOKS
THEOLOGY
THEORY AND PRACTICE

"Master, we know that you are an honest man and teach the way of God in an honest way, and that you are not afraid of anyone, because a man's rank means nothing to you" (Mt 22:16).

T

TEACHER PREPARATION AND TRAINING

Although we have seen desperate recruiting announcements in parish bulletins claiming "Anyone can teach" ("and we need you today"), there must be a screening process for candidates in teacher-preparation programs and some evaluation of those who complete training. Adequate preparation and suitability for teaching are indispensable prerequisites for teacher-catechists who have major responsibilities for the development of Christian maturity in our students.

Good teacher-preparation involves two components—course and field work. Both must begin at the same time. The *NCD* lists as the first element in preparation, "Basic orientation and preparation, including instruction in theology, scripture, psychology, and catechetical techniques" (No. 213). Most diocesan offices, in their certification requirements, list the basic content needed by teachers, and suggest that time be given to studying materials and methods of teaching. Most programs, however, do not give sufficient emphasis to field work and the relationship of field-based study to experiential learning, an approach highly praised in other sections in the *NCD*.

The basic concept of having people learn by doing is common to medicine, social work, construction and mechanical trades, and most of the arts. In all these the new learner is initiated into the field by being given opportunities to observe, to touch, to do simple tasks so that theory and practice will be integrated.

Major studies in teacher education have repeatedly urged that all teacher training in the field be done as early as possible in the program. There is generally no major obstacle to utilizing this approach in our teacher-preparation programs for religious education. Most volunteers who are new to teaching will welcome the opportunity first to observe a class, to tutor, or to work in small groups. This experience will be most valuable when it is correlated to the course work or seminar time. The new teachers must be willing to study theory and to practice-teach under the supervision of the DRE or master teacher.

As the teacher-candidates are learning about catechetics, the instructor must utilize as many different teaching models as appropriate in the course work, and not be restricted to lectures alone. Catechists need to see the various methods used so they can vary their own methods of teaching.

A continuous teacher-training program with a field-based part offers the candidates who are beginning their preparation the opportunity to help out in the room. And it allows the DREs or master teachers an opportunity to evaluate the candidates' ability and desire to teach. In some cases they may find a candidate not suitable for teaching. Such advance screening eliminates requesting resignations later.

Teacher preparation is a complex and difficult task. Obviously the work of any program is dependent on the quality of the staff. The truism, As you sow, so shall you reap, should be the guide and caution to all who seek shortcut solutions to teacher shortages.

TEAM TEACHING

The team approach is one way to handle a problem in religious education. Dioceses provide assistance to parish programs through resource teams. Specialists in such areas as theology, education and psychology visit parish religious education programs to assess needs, help solve problems and offer professional assistance. These teams also offer lectures and workshops for teaching catechists at regional congresses.

Team teaching at the parish level provides opportunities for both teachers and students. But it is not simply the presence of more than one teacher in a room at the same time, nor two teachers alternating sessions. It is interaction of two or more teachers with students, all working to integrate the whole learning experience. This obviously is difficult and requires cooperation and care in planning and practice.

Some of the positive aspects of the approach are: sharing skills, talents and experiences; providing a broader range of resources; offering more opportunities for teacher/student exchanges; sharing responsibility for planning, testing and evaluating.

One of the difficulties of team teaching is finding the additional time for common lesson preparation. Also it calls for each teacher to learn to share in the process of working with a group. Teachers on teams must become active observers who join in times of listening, discussing and doing. In their cooperative planning, team members must make an effort to take advantage of the best each has to offer the students. Specific areas of responsibility must be decided upon during the planning, but in practice the plan must be carried out flexibly. Perhaps the most critical problem is finding a team whose members have compatible values and attitudes toward learning, and who are willing to cooperate and share.

This whole approach depends upon the number of teacher-catechists available and the the skill of the DRE in helping form teams. Two teachers having difficulty teaching on their own are not good candidates. Teams must be prepared for the experience through observations of working teams, if possible, and through positive experiences in teaching alone.

TEXTBOOKS

Religion textbooks are catechetical tools that should be chosen to meet the needs of the students who will be using them. While textbooks usually come in a series, each volume must be judged on its own merits.

Some questions that teaching catechists should ask about the text they are using are:

▸ Do students like the textbook?

▸ Does it stimulate interest?

▸ Is it geared to the developmental levels of the learners?

▸ Is the vocabulary appropriate to student reading levels?

▸ Are the graphics, music, art and activities related to the themes and appealing to the students?

▸ Is the text appropriate for the students' socioeconomic and educational backgrounds?

▸ Does the text reflect post-Vatican II theology?

▸ Does it present the Christian message joyfully?

▸ Does it integrate scripture, doctrine, liturgy and morality in a manner appropriate to the age of the students?

▸ Does it avoid racism, sexism and narrow provincialism?

▸ Does the teacher's manual or edition suggest ideas for the best use of the text?

▸ Does the text encourage experiential and discovery learning?

▸ Does it provoke thought and discussion?

▸ Does it use a wide variety of lesson approaches?

▸ Is it a CCD or a Catholic school edition?

▸ Is there a parent component?

▸ Are there suggestions for home activities?

The best religion textbooks are only as good as the teacher makes them. There is no substitute for good teaching.

Some practical suggestions for catechists using textbooks with their classes are:

Do

▸ Familiarize yourself with the student text and the other components—manual, parents' notes, activity books, charts and records.

▸ Find out in advance whether or not the books belong to the students, can be written in or can be taken home.

▸ Have extra texts available for students who forgot or lost their copy.

▸ Evaluate each lesson.

Don't

▸ Be a slave to the text.

▸ Use the text as a reader.

▸ Make the text the only tool.

▸ Use the text without the teacher's manual.

See also MANUALS FOR TEACHERS, LESSON PLANS and HOMEWORK.

THEOLOGY

Not long ago theology and catechetics were almost totally separate disciplines. The vital interaction between content and method needed for religious education was lacking.

Today theology and catechetics are more complementary. According to the *NCD*, "Catechesis draws on theology, and theology draws in turn on the richness of the Church's catechetical experience. Both must be at the service of the Church" (No. 37).

Theology, the study of the nature of God and religious truth, works toward a richer understanding of the gospel message. It does so by systematic and scholarly methods, using philosophy, history and other studies to understand and express Christian truths more clearly.

Catechetics draws from theology, and also from scripture, liturgy and the social sciences, not for reflection, but to move individuals and communities to mature expressions of faith.

How do they interact? Catechists draw upon the work of theologians as one of the resources needed in religious education to bring students to a fuller understanding of their Christian life.

Catechetics has provided a continuing and living source of how Christ's message has been received, absorbed and practiced. In catechetical experiences doctrine is tested for its meaning to God's people. Also from the presence of the Spirit in the lives and practices of the Christian community, theologians draw an understanding of the content of God's message.

The Christian faith is often most fully expressed in the interaction of scholars and community, both refining and clarifying through prayer, study and practice what it means to be people of faith.

Today the sources of belief, as formally worked out by theologians, are more and more available to teaching catechists. Schools of theology, seminaries and universities are providing summer workshops, pastoral institutes, weekend classes (both credit and non-credit) for teacher-catechists.

As theology and catechetics receive from each other, they have also greatly improved their effectiveness. In theology today there is a richer and more practical pastoral and catechetical dimension, and in religious education we are absorbing the fuller theological traditions of the church.

THEORY AND PRACTICE

The explosion in religious education theory, precipitated by such thinkers as Hofinger, Jungmann, Sloyan, Nebrada, Babin and Moran, and described in *Resurgence of Religious Instruction* (Religious Education Press), has subsided. The wave, begun in the 1950s, seemed to crest in the 1960s with some flow into the 1970s. Contemporary catechetics seems to be on a plateau. Today's insights about the role of scripture, doctrine, liturgy, morality, methodology and educational psychology derive from those years that radically changed the direction of catechetics. Church documents, such as the Second Vatican Council's *Declaration on Christian Education*, the National Conference of Catholic Bishops' publication *To Teach As Jesus Did* and the *NCD*, all confirm the influence of these authors and encourage further thinking and research.

In practice we are still coming to grips with the implications of the theory developed in the past 25 years. There are many openings to the future developed in the past 25 years. There are many openings to the future, but it might seem to some that a unified thrust is lacking in catechetics today. In the earlier years there were common discoveries about scripture, changes in the liturgy and explorations of educational theory. After these discoveries came the need to place them into a context that all could recognize.

Teachers are involved in the application of what theory has to offer. They are the ones who face the task of teaching a regular group of students. Here, practice must call upon what is now endorsed in the *NCD* and continue what is commonly referred to as the good sense aspect of teaching—careful preparation, knowledge of students, acceptance of the teaching of the community. All this demands the prudent action of the teacher who must deal with the present and who uses what is now available and has proven effective.

In religious education/catechetics, teachers need the research and ideas of the theorists. (In some cases it was the practitioner who gave the first sign of new thinking.) In contemporary catechetics new voices are needed; in the interim we need to hold on to what has been given, work it out and hope that the forces of theory and practice both crest again.

U

Ungraded Programs
(see GRADE-LEVEL SYSTEM)

V

VALUES CLARIFICATION
VOLUNTEERS

W

Workshops
(see IN-SERVICE TRAINING)

"If you make my word your home
you will indeed be my disciples,
you will learn the truth
and the truth will make you free" (Jn 8:31-32).

V

VALUES CLARIFICATION

There is an old Indian adage that says, It is better to teach a hungry man to fish than to give him a fish. Teachers are in the business of preparing students to evaluate, interpret, judge and decide—not of handing out answers or ready-made solutions.

Much has been written today about the need to help students acquire the skills to survive in a changing world. Values clarification, a technique based on the work of Louis Raths and carried out by Sidney Simon, is one attempt to improve the thinking and valuing skills of students. These authors propose approaches to teach the process of valuing and have devised methods to help people establish a hierarchy of values upon which they can make decisions.

According to Raths and Simon, values are formed when a person freely chooses from available alternatives, and understands the consequences of choosing each alternative. Some of the techniques are game-like and students find them interesting and enjoyable. Among the more commonly used are:

rank order	helps students develop a hierarchy of things most valuable to them.
value sheets	offer provocative statements with clarifying questions that require students' written responses.
"I learned" statements	ask students to pick out key ideas from a lesson or experience, and confirm or decide on their value.
forced choice	puts students in situations where decisions must be made.
value voting, survey or grid	makes students reflect, through comparison, on their own or others' values.

Many religious educators utilize values-clarification techniques to help students discover and accept the values of the Christian community. As the students grow in their ability to sort out information and values, and to see creative alternatives, they will become reflective decision makers.

Jesus continually challenged his listeners to think out choices, to make comparisons, and to act on what they thought. He told the sick young man, "If you would be perfect, go sell what you have and follow me."

The *NCD* asks religious educators to do more than give answers:

> As children mature, catechesis does more to help them observe, explore, interpret, and judge their experiences, ascribe a Christian meaning to their lives, and act according to the norms of faith and love. The presence in today's society of many conflicting values makes it all the more important to help young people to interiorize authentic values (No. 181).

This is a call to an active process for both teachers and the students. The words used are *observe, explore, interpret, judge, ascribe,* and *act*—all to *norms* of faith and love. This requires time, patience and caution, on the part of teacher-catechists who choose this approach.

The *NCD* further states in its guidelines for children and youth that

> constructive interaction and personal involvement are extremely important, and are present in gospel-based value clarification, group discussions, programs for the development of communication skills and group prayer (No. 181).

VOLUNTEERS

Volunteers are the backbone of most religious education programs today, especially with the decline of traditional religious vocations. Increasingly volunteers teach, plan liturgies, organize service groups and study programs, generally in collaboration with the DRE or a member of the parish staff. In some cases, however, the religious education programs are actually directed by volunteers and fully staffed by them.

The *NCD* advises that volunteers be prepared for their work through special programs designed to help them acquire the knowledge and skills needed to fulfill their tasks. Instruction must be given in theology, scripture, psychology, liturgy, morality and catechetical techniques.

Since volunteers make a commitment to serve as catechists, the parish has the obligation to match that commitment with real support such as financial backing, use of parish facilities, provision of resources and coordination of religious education programs with other parish activities. It must also make efforts to encourage and acknowledge work well done. The attitudes toward volunteers, of the pastor, assistants, the DRE and the religious serving the parish community, are critical to the success of the program. In general, if the program is viewed as run by "only volunteers" who are substitutes for professionals, there will be a conflict. If the volunteer is accepted as a dedicated member of the parish who shares time, talent and effort for a community endeavor, the program will be the basis for a major growth in parish life.

See also COMMUNITY.

Y

YOUTH MINISTRY

Z

ZACCHAEUS

"Teacher, we want to see you work some signs" (Mt 12:38, NAB).

Y

YOUTH MINISTRY

Youth Ministry is an approach now being used to help change the attitude that a once-a-week religion class is all there is to offer the young people of a parish. Youth Ministry is an attempt to provide a total ministry, including catechesis, to junior and senior high school students.

The *NCD* stresses the need for a variety of approaches in ". . . preparing social, recreational, and apostolic programs, as well as retreats and other spiritual-development activities" (No. 228).

Youth Ministry models vary with the needs of young people from parish to parish. Through them many more young adults and adolescents can be reached than through catechetical programs that are simply classroom sessions. In a comprehensive program, instruction is part of the overall structure that includes opportunities to foster community, celebrate liturgies, offer service, participate in parish activities, receive guidance and share prayer experiences.

For those planning youth programs the *NCD* guidelines suggest that "professional advice, local initiative and consultation with young people themselves" should all go into the planning process (No. 228). There are programs for the preparation of youth ministers which assist in exploring various models of ministry, help set up youth leadership training programs, and offer some insights about youth—their developmental characteristics, their interests and needs. Certain qualifications are needed by all youth ministers. They must genuinely like being with young people, sharing their time, ideas and talents with them. And they must accept with patience and understanding the problems of adolescents.

Teacher-catechists involved in youth ministry must be part of the whole approach and not just isolated classroom teachers. Decisions about the type of curriculum to be followed, frequency and location of classes, whether the sessions will be formal or informal, must all be made in conjunction with the overall program.

A *National Inventory of Parish Catechetical Programs* (United States Catholic Conference) offers some picture of youth-ministry programs in parishes today. It notes that the most common services provided for youth by parishes are: 1) organized sports; 2) use of a youth center; and 3) counselling. Many parishes report they never have scripture study groups, paraliturgies or retreats. And about a quarter of the parishes responding never have eucharistic celebrations or penance services for youth.

Young people can serve the parish as members of the parish council, as catechists, catechist aides, musicians for liturgies, and extraordinary ministers of the Eucharist. They can also become involved in community service and action for justice.

Some references for youth ministers:

A Vision of Youth Ministry is a publication of the Department of Education of the United States Catholic Conference (USCC). *Catholic Youth Ministry* includes a cassette tape and packet and is issued six times a year (Catholic Youth Ministry).

Other books include: *Portrait of Youth Ministry* and *Resources for Youth Ministry* (Paulist Press); *Parish Youth Ministry* (Twenty-Third Publications); and *The Junior Highs* (St. Mary's College Press).

Prime Time is two cassette tapes with a guide (NCR cassettes).

See also HIGH SCHOOL PROGRAMS, JUNIOR HIGH SCHOOL PROGRAMS, ADOLESCENTS, DEVELOPMENTAL PSYCHOLOGY and SEXUALITY.

Z

ZACCHAEUS

Zacchaeus (Lk 19:1-10) is a model for
catechists. He was resourceful enough to take
the means at hand in order to get to see Jesus.
In the words of *The New England Primer*,

Zacheus he
Did Climb the Tree
His Lord to see.

Jesus Our Teacher

Seeing the crowds, he went up the hill. There he sat down and was joined by his disciples. Then he began to speak. This is what he taught them:

> "How happy are the poor in spirit;
> theirs is the kingdom of heaven.
> Happy the *gentle:*
> *they shall have the earth for their heritage.*
> Happy those who mourn:
> they shall be comforted.
> Happy those who hunger and thirst for what is right:
> they shall be satisfied.
> Happy the merciful:
> they shall have mercy shown them.
> Happy the pure in heart:
> they shall see God.
> Happy the peacemakers:
> they shall be called sons of God.
> Happy those who are persecuted in the cause of right:
> theirs is the kingdom of heaven.

"Happy are you when people abuse you and persecute you and speak all kinds of calumny against you on my account. Rejoice and be glad, for your reward will be great in heaven; this is how they persecuted the prophets before you" (Mt 5:1-12).

NOTES

(Diocesan resources and personnel; programs, workshops, conferences; publishers' materials and representatives; available teaching aids and other equipment; lists of volunteers; etc.)

NOTES

NOTES

NOTES